*Under
Running Laughter*

Under Running Laughter

Notes from a Renegade Classroom

Quincy Howe, Jr.

THE FREE PRESS
A Division of Macmillan, Inc.
NEW YORK
Collier Macmillan Canada
TORONTO
Maxwell Macmillan International
NEW YORK OXFORD SINGAPORE SYDNEY

The Free Press
A Division of Macmillan, Inc.
866 Third Avenue, New York, N.Y. 10022

Collier Macmillan Canada, Inc.
1200 Eglinton Avenue East
Suite 200
Don Mills, Ontario M3C 3N1

Printed in the United States of America

printing number
1 2 3 4 5 6 7 8 9 10

Library of Congress Cataloging-in-Publication Data

Howe, Quincy
    Under running laughter : notes from a renegade classroom
/ Quincy Howe, Jr.
        p.   cm.
    Includes index.
    ISBN 0-02-915293-3
    1. Socially handicapped children—Education
(Secondary)—New York (N.Y.)—Case studies. 2. Education,
Urban—New York (N.Y.)—Case studies.   3. Leake & Watts
High School (New York, N.Y.)   4. Remedial teaching—New
York (N.Y.)—Case studies.   5. Howe, Quincy,
date.   6. Teachers of socially handicapped children—New
York (N.Y.)—Biography.   I. Title.
LC4093.N5H69   1990
371.96'7'097471—dc20   90-40511
                                                  CIP

For Esther

Contents

Acknowledgments

I wish to thank the following persons for their help during the preparation of this book:

Thomas Dunnings, of the Manuscript Library of the New York Historical Society, assisted me with the archival material on the history of Leake & Watts.

Selma K. Levy, Director of Education at Leake & Watts, helped expedite my manuscript through the agency's administration and Board of Trustees.

Tom Wallace, my agent, was cool and confident at times when I was not.

Susan Adler, a sensitive reader and a serious combatant in the helping services, gave me editorial guidance and encouragement from start to finish.

Joyce Seltzer, my editor at The Free Press, helped me to find sense and continuity in the moody and amorphous manuscript I turned in to her.

Above all, my wife Esther never failed to encourage me and make time available for writing, often at her own inconvenience.

Prologue

> Who if I were to cry would hear me
> from the orders of angels?
>
> —*Rilke*, Duino Elegies

This is a book about children whom no one heard when they cried. The children at Leake & Watts are in foster care, some at their own request, some at the request of their families, and some at the insistence of the courts. What they all have in common is a broken and defective family life. Having been abused, neglected, and unloved as young children, they have grown up into adolescents who are angry, unmanageable, and at odds with society.

Leake & Watts is an agency that has been taking care of orphaned and abandoned children for over 150 years. It is a private residential facility that is paid by the city and state of New York to provide a home and schooling for about 90 children from the ages of 10 to 20. The children are all from the city of New York and they are predominantly black. It is in the Leake & Watts High School that I have my contact with them.

The experience of trying to teach the children has been both moving and exasperating, but above all it has been engrossing. I am always aware that I am immersed in a social problem of unparalleled magnitude and complexity.

Although I can lose myself almost entirely in the day-to-day business of coaxing, cajoling, and horsing around with my students, I find that there is a part of my mind that stands apart and asks with uncomprehending dismay what can be done both for the present generation and for the ones that will follow. The self-esteem of these students is abject, their capacity for sustained effort is limited, their grasp of the world that awaits them is fragmentary and askew, their social skills are crude.

I am teaching children who were born less than 30 blocks from the apartment where I was raised in New York City, and yet

1

their world is so different from mine they could have come from a different continent. Upon becoming acquainted with them and with their personal histories, I feel that the ease and comfort of my own life are diminished by the desperate lives they lead.

The impetus to write this book arose abruptly after I had been teaching at Leake & Watts for about four months. It was the Friday before Martin Luther King Day and we were holding a service in the agency's chapel to commemorate the legacy of Dr. King. The children read excerpts from Dr. King's speeches and then the service concluded with everyone, staff and students, locking arms to sing "We Shall Overcome." I was unexpectedly moved, not by the humane optimism of the sixties, but by a sense of ineluctable tragedy. Not only had the generation of the sixties failed to overcome; here was another battered and demoralized generation whose prospects of overcoming are probably worse than they were 25 years ago.

To see how these children struggle against their various impediments, and to join in the task of trying to assist them, is to step into a piteous arena of human damage and inadequate resources. There is a way of writing about the underclass that depicts them as lively, charming, vivid, engaging—and all of these things are true of the children of Leake & Watts. To make light, however, of their anger, their intransigence, opposition, and general inability to master their own lives is to lose sight of their plight.

I do not claim that these lives are representative of the entire urban underclass. The abuse and neglect they have endured, however, is a heightened instance of the chaos and deprivation that is rife wherever a group is socially and economically isolated. In that sense their story does represent an important segment of life in our inner cities.

In writing about the children I have tried to maintain the voice and perspective of an educator. This is in fact probably the only voice I can maintain with any authority and conviction. Prior to coming to Leake & Watts I taught Greek and Latin on the college level for 15 years. One of the things that caused me to resign my tenure was my growing dissatisfaction with the divergence between education as it was understood in the ancient world and college education as it was understood in the 1970s. I had initially been drawn to the classics by the way in which Greek and Roman education addressed itself to the development of the entire person. After six good years and nine that were not so good I left in dismay over the decline of humanistic education and the concomitant rise of narrow specialization.

To work with the children of Leake & Watts is to position education at the center of human development to a higher degree than I ever thought possible. The term that most aptly describes the affliction of these children is undersocialization. By this I mean low self-regard, an undeveloped moral code, an oppositional style of dealing with other people, and abject expectations of the future. When education carries out its traditional and primal task, these are its proper areas of concern. Although I am not thinking of Homer, Plato, Cicero, and Virgil while teaching these students, I am aware that I am doing more than just imparting knowledge. The classic exemplar of the educator was Chiron the centaur who taught the Greek heroes fortitude, probity, rhetoric, music, and skill with arms. I spend the first three hours of every day with a group of adolescents to whom I teach language arts, mathematics, how to read a newspaper, how to process photographs, how to operate a computer, how to avoid venereal disease, how to use a sewing machine. I am also trying to teach them how to esteem themselves and others, how to accept adults as a benign influence in their lives, and how to prepare for a future whose shape is now ominous and confusing for them.

My students come from homes that have been ravaged by chaos, poverty, crime, drug addiction, and violence. Socially, culturally, educationally, and emotionally they are unfinished people. The psychiatrist, the therapist, the social worker can address a part of the job, but a teacher can address the entire job. By being with the children day after day, week after week, the teacher becomes a persistent reminder of hope, competence, progress, and self-mastery.

With oppositional children such as those at Leake & Watts the essential problem, undersocialization, is not a pathology but a deficit of nurture. If these children are going to be made whole again, it will be done through the unfailing attention of patient people who can say again and again, "Come into my classroom and let me help you grow." Probably the greatest moment in the school year is the first day of class in September. These children who customarily cursed at us, hurled their books on the floor, and stormed out of the room are boundlessly pleased to see their teachers again at the end of summer recess. From the girls there are crushing hugs and from the boys the exotic and artful handshakes that signify acceptance. We are the one group of adults who can always be counted on to be there and to give it all one more try.

On the uplifting side, the work of teaching these students is humane in the full sense of the word. On the distressing side, however, one's best efforts and ultimate exertions are insufficient to mend the damage that has been done. The children are so oppositional, the opportunity to work with them intensively so limited, the world that awaits them upon adulthood so unpromising, and the sheer human energy for the work in such short supply that the real job of enabling and rehabilitation gets done only in small and inadequate pieces.

To plan ahead, set goals, and complete significant pieces of instruction is impossible. In the course of a day's work one simply meets more children with more needs and in less time than the job allows. As a result, one is always denied the satisfaction of getting a job done and looking on a finished piece of work. There is nothing here that compares with teaching a college undergraduate for four years and ending up with a promising young scholar. Even when one does overcome a child's resistance and attains some degree of compliance and affection, the progress is so gradual, subtle, and subliminal that one is really not aware of it. To endure and persist at this work requires that one be willing to go on without the reassurance of visible results.

And yet, the work is strangely energizing. If the mind is disengaged from progressing toward some quantifiable objective, one can then give one's self over to the immediacy of the moment. Every work imposes its particular discipline, and the discipline of this work is paying attention. The more one pays attention to the anger, opposition, and depression of these children, the more these conditions subside. At its best this work offers a reckless and consuming absorption with the passing moment. At its worst the mind reels and staggers back from the abyss of inner chaos that afflicts these children.

My students are the victims of a past that has left them with a potent charge of anger and opposition. Their outbursts of violence, abusive language, and general contentiousness constitute an attempt to relieve some of this negative energy. If those who work with them can simply stand by and absorb some of these jolts of energy, the process of socialization will be set in motion. Further, if one can approach the children with openness, intensity, and affection—without dwelling inordinately on the teaching that is not getting done, the rules that are being broken, the classes that are being disrupted—then the work can become expansive and liberating.

The immediate problem of the children I teach is some recent rejection or abuse from a parent or parent-surrogate. Behind that is chaotic and deprived family life extending back at least two generations. And behind that is a degree of social isolation and economic hardship that has cut off the inner city underclass from the prosperity and comfort that surround them.

When faced by the problems of crime, drug addiction, inner city unemployment, gratuitous violence, fragmentary families, and low-level job skills, those charged with helping these children are overwhelmed and reduced to a sense of impotence. To solve the problems of the children of Leake & Watts is to solve a cluster of social problems that have been with us for several decades and are growing worse. Our sense of impotence nurtures a pernicious tendency to set short-term goals and to make the care custodial rather than truly regenerative.

There is more to my job than the queer exhilaration that accompanies exceedingly difficult work performed under straitened circumstances. In order to carry on from day to day I need to cultivate an attitude of reckless indifference toward success and failure. To succumb entirely to this attitude, however, is to fail my students and the generation that will follow them. I am now caught in the precarious dilemma between hanging on and letting go which I believe lies at the heart of any attempt to teach.

Is the business of conveying information from one person to another really worthy of being called teaching? Even under the best of conditions, does an inspired teacher really enlighten a receptive student? And what about those less than ideal conditions where the students refuse to be educated and the teacher sees his hopes and expectations mocked and thwarted? My own belief, which has been fortified by my four years at Leake & Watts, is that behind all the attempted instruction and clash of wills there exists, independent of both the teacher and the student, a benign tendency of human nature to better itself. The teacher's position is precarious because there is no sure way of knowing whether you are blocking or assisting that benign tendency, especially with children as profoundly dispirited as those I teach.

1

The Children of Leake & Watts

My home in the Bronx is a little more than half-a-mile from Leake & Watts, which means that I am one of those fortunate New Yorkers who can walk to work. No matter how bleak the weather or how forbidding the prospect of facing my students for yet another day, my disposition takes a momentary turn for the better as I enter the grounds of the agency. The school, the residential cottages, and the administrative building occupy a magnificent stretch of land in south Yonkers overlooking the Hudson River. Formerly a farm, the grounds were sold to Leake & Watts in 1887, as the soil was too salty to be readily arable. The original main building, which is still in use, is made of yellow brick with reddish sandstone trim around the windows. It has arches and parapets over the main entrance and exudes a *beaux arts* concern for accent and detail. The buildings, however, are an adjunct to the grounds, which were laid out by Frederick Law Olmstead, the designer of New York City's Central Park. Like Central Park, the grounds represent an attempt to enlist nature's exuberance without subduing it. The terrain slopes down from the main administrative building in gentle undulations. About a dozen ancient trees—

sycamores, willows, and pines—are strategically positioned so as to scatter a pattern of mottled shade over the entire grounds.

I walk past the residential cottages at about 8:10, some 20 minutes before the children are required to be in school. From the open windows I hear rap music and bickering voices. By the time I have passed the four cottages that lie on either side of my route to the school, several students have called out from behind drawn curtains: "What's up, Howe?" "Save me a piece of candy, Howe." "Hey, Howe, what's happening?" Many of these children have been at the agency two or three years, so I know them by their voices and can answer back by name.

The day ahead may appear daunting and difficult, but these voices remind me that my role as teacher and their role as students is the veneer beneath which other graver matters are resolving themselves. This is their home, and I am quite literally walking through their front yard. Their calls and my answers bespeak a connection that runs deeper than the vicissitudes of the classroom. I am entering a setting in which for more than 100 years displaced children have sought to find coherence, affection, and hope.

Behind the main building the grounds slope abruptly down toward the Hudson River. About half-way down to the river there is a flat stretch of land where the high school is situated. As I look down to the school, I can see the river as well as the palisades on the opposite shore; seagulls are generally circling overhead.

Once I get down to the building, I have about 15 minutes to steady my nerves before the students arrive. Most of my colleagues are in the teachers' lounge, taking their uneasy pleasure over a cup of coffee and waiting with apprehension for 8:30, when the children begin to come in.

I arrive at school each morning with the pockets of my jacket—I always wear a coat and tie and am the only teacher who does so—bulging with candy. As the children arrive, I pass the candies out with careless profligacy to all students, wild and docile, just to let it be known that the prevailing code of rewarding only good conduct does not necessarily apply in all instances. My colleagues look on with curious indulgence, as this flies in the face of the behaviorist principles generally applied in this field of education.

I try to maintain this bravado throughout the day, but generally end up being deflated and overwhelmed by the pervasive presence of pain and opposition.

More than anything else, my day is a sequence of frustration, chastisement, verbal abuse, and sardonic laughter. To the extent that I take all of this seriously, enter into eye contact, raise my voice—to that extent these children are engaged and affected by what is going on. The art of teaching them, as I see it, is to be at once lighthearted and intensely involved. One of the leading psychoanalytic writers on child development, D. W. Winnicott, has posited that acting out behavior is an expression of hope—hope that one will be recognized and noticed at last. I feel that the morning candies are a way of recognizing this hope. The students are generally happiest when they are acting out and receiving a response. Thus I find that teaching them is something of a balancing act wherein one tries to maintain their ebullience, impose limits on their excesses, and impart information—all at the same time.

The children's demands and anxieties create an extraordinary challenge for a teacher. As I work with them, I am constantly trying to take the measure of their needs. Are they able to grasp how the past has determined the present? What expectations do they entertain for the future? Do they see themselves as sinned against? Do they view placement in Leake & Watts as an opportunity to reassemble the broken pieces of their lives? There is a tentative answer to these questions to be found in the essays, reports, and letters the children have written for me in school over the past few years. Some of these came into being as class assignments; others were desperate missives sent off to the world at large with no special prompting. Although some passages may seem overdone and exaggerated, the composite picture to emerge from my students' writings is consistent both with the histories in their clinical files and with the accounts of inner-city life in the newspaper.

One of the first things that becomes evident to anyone who spends any time with the children is how much they enjoy their own mischief. Far from being stricken by remorse and regret, they get rousing satisfaction from breaking rules, affronting others, and leaving a broad wake of outrage and indignation. When no serious harm is done, the pranks and insults can be charged with an engaging vitality and humor.

When the students do a writing assignment, they are often flattered by my interest in how bad they can be. The following three pieces exude the delight they experience in being bad. An exceedingly difficult girl, Sondra B, who was at our school for about a year, was smart, but simply refused to do any school work. I finally asked her to give me advice on how to curse people out, and this is what she came up with.

> There is only a few things I could say about cursing people out. 1. You have to say a lot of cursing like bitch, asshole, skeezer, sluts, etc. 2. You have to say it real loud and you only do this to people that you don't like or hate. For instance, if they are stupid, you just tell them that they are stupid.
> But if they get smart, that's when you curse them out. If they dis you, call them all kinds of whores, slut, bitch, etc.
> And if they dis your family you curse them out and beat the shit out of them. And if they steal from you, you call them a no good stinking bum and beat the shit out of them. And if they mess with your boy or girl friend, you call them all kinds of skeezer and wax their ass.
> That's how I would curse them out.

This may strike the gentle reader as a gratuitous and repetitive display of foul language. For many of my students, however, the first day of trouble in school had occurred six or eight years earlier when they said to a teacher, "Fuck this shit. I'm not doing it."

The following piece, also by Sondra, was her response to my assignment for a description of "The Wildest Person I Knew."

> The wildest person I knew is Roseann. She be doing a lot of crazy shit, like one day me and Roseann was in the bus going to the Bronx and I took this girl umbrella and I give it to Roseann. Then this other white girl was getting off the bus. She asked us for the umbrella and we said we didn't have it. Then she try to take it from Roseann so she threw it at her. So she start calling us stupid black niggers and bitches, so Roseann spit on her and the girl started to run after the bus and we start laughing real hard. On the bus Roseann was laughing real loud.
> I also remember one day me and Roseann was walking down the street and I pull this girl hair and Roseann come out of nowhere and beat the living shit out of her and I kick the girl in her ass. There is plenty more to tell, but I can't remember it right now.

Therapists who depend on a child's pain and discomfort with his or her behavior would find really very little to go on here. I will occasionally try to call my students to account when they beat up another child, and they will just laugh at my remonstrances. "Man, that stupid, funky bum deserved an asskicking. Next time he gets two asskickings." When these children are on an antic high, they are not troubled by the stings of conscience.

Here is a letter we have all wanted to write at one time or another. In a preparatory exercise for the New York State Regents Competency Test in writing, one phase of which is the writing of a conventional and correct business letter, I ask my students to express a grievance over a defective piece of audio equipment.

> *1888 Flatbush Ave.*
> *Brooklyn, NY 10509*
> *7/1/87*
>
> *Sony of America*
> *8600 East Main St.*
> *Reynoldsburg, OH 43068*
>
> *Dear Sirs:*
>
> *I would like to send back the TV/Radio I bought from you because it is a piece of shit. The name is Sony Model #206. And you better send my money back as soon as you get this letter.*
>
> *Sincerely yours,*
>
> *P.S. If I don't get my money back I'm going to kill your dog, meaning your wife.*

The writer handed it to me with such purposeful solemnity that I knew something was up. He got his desired result—I laughed. And I got what I wanted—when the test came two months later, he passed. I am often caught in the paradox of being so amused by my students' mischief that I do not take serious steps to correct it.

It is when the children write about their homes and life on the streets that one sees the flawed foundations upon which their lives stand. As I teach them, I try not to think of the quality of life to which they will return once their schooling is over. The traditional function of foster care was to take in, shelter, and rear a child who lacked an appropriate home. The desired outcome was to discharge the child to a viable environment in which to deploy viable job skills. And for the first 100 years this is basically what was happening at Leake & Watts. There was a school on the grounds, there was an agency-owned farm upstate, and there was vocational training within the local community. Upon reaching the age of 16 the children were either apprenticed out or sent off to college.

All of this was predicated on sending the children out into a stable and supportive community. At the present time, the quality of life of the underclass in the inner city makes this a virtual impossibility. Never have unemployment, drug abuse, violent crime, the numbers of out-of-wedlock children, and socioeconomic isolation been worse.

We tend, however, to suppress our uneasy awareness that any hope of turning these children into competent and autonomous adults demands that they do *not* return to the scene of their rearing. Here is what I would take to be a typical narrative of neighborhood life in Queens. It was submitted by one of my students under the title, "Life in the Crack Lane."

> Life in Queens is not as quiet as people say it is. South Jamaica is always live. There are crack dealers everywhere. I have seen niggers get beat down over crack. My friends sell crack and they don't like losing their money.
>
> One Saturday night Pee Wee had this box outside while he was selling. So this kid named Dwayne was out there. He took five hundred dollars worth of crack and the box behind Pee Wee's back. Pee Wee and the rest of the dealers had to pay for the crack, and Pee Wee had to buy a new box.
>
> So on Sunday morning I was looking out the window of my god sister house Annette, my cousin Nancy, and I were going across the street to the store. Pee Wee, Boney, Born, Ralph, and Dwayne was standing on the corner. So Pee Wee back slapped Dwayne.
>
> They took Dwayne across the street to the park. Pee Wee picked up a wood stick and started beating Dwayne with it. They started beating him at 11:30. Born came at around 12:30. So Born told Pee Wee to keep Dwayne in the park. He said to Dwayne, "Boy, you ain't going no where, we whipping your ass all day."
>
> By Dimples

What is going to happen to a 16-year-old girl who is going to be sent back to the streets where Dwayne and Pee Wee are "whipping ass" all day over a crack theft? A hundred years ago, radical social interventions were available. Many orphans were sent to the western frontier where they were taken in as foster children in return for their labor. The truly incorrigible ones would be sent off on a whaling voyage which could last as long as two years. Centuries earlier, in the late Roman Republic and early Empire, the government was able to relieve the problem of the urban proletariat by giving them land to homestead in the provinces. These solutions are possible, however, only for an expanding country with uncultivated regions. Today, once treatment has ended, the range of possibilities extends only up to Yonkers and then back down to the Bronx or Brooklyn.

The original model of mental health care is the middle class ministering to the middle class. What happens, however, when the patient has experienced a degree of chaos and deprivation that lies beyond the comprehension of those who would help? Here is an account, written in serial form, of a couple of weekend passes to Brooklyn:

> It started like this. The weekend before last I went to the movie with a friend of mine, and I pull out some money as this kid name Tut that my brother know snatched forty dollars from me and I told him that he had to see me again.
>
> So this weekend I went home. That night I went to a party and these kids were there. So I called them outside. Then my cousin started to fight one of them. While he was fighting, it seemed like the whole building came outside. The odds were uneven.
>
> So we started to walk away. This kid named Shado kept saying, "Y'all don't want no pressure."
>
> So I said, "You don't want a war you can't fuck with." So after that they threw a tin can at us. So we kept walking. When we got under a tunnel Shado pulled out a 25 automatic and started to shoot me in the back. So I pull out the 357 Magnum and passed it to my friend Shagod. He started to shoot back. Their gun compared to ours sounded like a cap gun.
>
> So I was running and I didn't see the gate. So I kept running until I ran into the gate. Everybody who was with me thought I was shot until I started to run again. So it was over for the day.
>
> Monday I told my man that I had to go to my aunt house (that's where the beef was going on) so I told him if I'm not back in fifteen minutes something is wrong.

So I was not back. K-Born and V came looking for me. They saw one of those niggers who was down with the shit and blits on him. So the kid started to run and he turn around and bust one at K-Born and V. So K-Born pull out and start to shoot at him. So that is it until next week.

As far as I know, the curriculum that can engage and socialize such a student has not yet been created. At some point even the most magnanimous system has to draw the line between the possible and the impossible. And then those who are found to be incorrigible graduate to schools of harder and harder knocks. Common sense dictates spending as much as possible as early as possible, before the liability of the difficult child grows into the much greater liability of the adult criminal.

The resources, however, that might turn around the writer of the quoted passage were not available when he was with us. It was evident that he was one of our brighter students, and I hoped that individual attention might engage him. Our school principal gave me *carte blanche* to take two students aside and make a yearbook. While working with him my mind would wander to the things I knew about his career on the streets. Could I seriously expect someone who had spent the weekend dodging bullets to give me his undivided attention for a high school yearbook? My misgivings were well warranted: within two weeks he could no longer endure the expectations and the requirement to produce and he stopped showing up. He left the agency within a year and was seen on school grounds a few months after his discharge; he was carrying a pistol and driving a stolen car.

Generally our most difficult students are the ones whose families have been in the city for a couple of generations. Once the pattern of child neglect has become established as a recurring fact of family history, the appropriate remedy is something far more radical than anything we have come up with yet. What intervention can speak to a child who is prepared to risk his life for $40? For a teacher to talk to such students about growth, development, and the future, there needs to be a consensus between students and teacher that these are realities.

The next piece was written by a sweet-tempered young man, co-editor of the ill-fated yearbook. He was raised in the South and then came to a broken family in New York shortly before adolescence. At an age when many of our boys were snatching chains and purses, he was down in South Carolina learning how to slaughter and dress a hog.

> There is a variety of people on my block, such as homos, Spanish, black, Caucasians, sellers, crack heads, stickup kids, and freaks. Freaks are hot tamales.
>
> We pass the time by taking the #4 train to 149th Street where we get off and pick up my cousin. Then we get back on the 4 train to 125 Street. We walk to 127 Street and Madison where I pick up my other cousin. That's when we pick up the SES [drugs] and go to 42nd Street to see a movie. I like my neighborhood because there are lots of athletes who give me comp (competition). What I do not like about my neighborhood is that Spanish crackheads go around shooting my friends.

Unlike the writer of the previous piece, this young man has a bemused sense of distance from the street scene. He is more of a tourist than a participant. I attribute this to his southern origins, and in fact I find that our students who have had some of their rearing in the South are more tractable and less damaged by the chaos of street life. Although he was uncontrollably silly and childish during his stay at Leake & Watts, he graduated, spent a semester at one of the city colleges on an athletic scholarship, and then dropped out to enlist in the Navy. The last time I saw him, he had just finished basic training and all the foolishness of his school days was gone. He is now stationed overseas and sent me a Christmas card in which he wished me season's greetings and informed me that the time had come for the legacy of Malcolm X to assert itself.

The following piece is by a girl who was simply too wild for us to help. She left the agency before her time was up, pregnant by another resident, and in fact has come back a couple of times to show off her baby.

> My sister and friends be having weapons due to the fact that there are a lot of jealous girls out there to fight for no reason at all. My sister be carrying knives, My cousin be carrying axes and some carry razor blades and some carry guns.
>
> The reason why they carry all these things is because people out there be wanting to kill you over jealousy. So, instead of them killing you, you kill them.

When you want to use a razor blade, you have to slice them on the face or across the chest or back. And if you are really mean, you try to kill them.

When my cousin and me have weapons, we go for the kill. We aim for the neck or vein, and I'm vicious so I go for the neck.

The girls in Brooklyn are crazy jealous, so they be wanting to kill you for no reason at all. But as I see it, I'll go for kill before they kill me.

One of the areas where we have real success with our residents is subduing some of the violence in their lives. Although they are constantly getting into verbal exchanges that culminate in promises of knives, guns, and pieces of pipe, this does not happen. They become quickly aware of the fact that in order to maintain their honor at Leake & Watts they do not have to live up to the street code of relentless violence. And they are greatly relieved at this.

The writer of this piece, however, was constantly AWOL and never really succeeded in shedding the street culture. If we could have just kept her at Leake & Watts and off the streets, we would have been performing a significant service; even this purely custodial task, however, turned out to be impossible.

Once these children have been removed from a criminalized or abusive home, how do they feel about coming to a residential agency? Do they see it as an opportunity to advance their lives, or do they see it as another desperate way station on a slippery path? Here is one view:

My worst experience was to move into a group home or to move into an institution like Leake & Watts. This institution is for people who are not able to cope with problems that they are having in their homes or in their schools. I do not feel that I should be here because I feel that I can cope with the problems at home or in my school.

I am sitting here typing this in my classroom and my class is one of the worst in the entire world. I do not belong here because of the fact that I can do a lot better than anyone else in this school.

I want to go home, but because my mother is so stubborn I really would settle to stay right where I am.

I guess I will be signing off now because I have to go, but until the next time take care and I will speak to you soon.

I reflect with mixed feelings that I shall be remembered as presiding over a class that "is one of the worst in the world." Typical of all of our students are the mixed feelings of rancor and resignation. The writer of this piece is outraged at having ended up in placement ("My worst experience") and yet he feels impotent to change his situation ("I really would settle to stay right where I am").

The writer was one our brightest students—bright enough to be talented at getting into trouble. He was forced to leave within less than a year for taking an agency van and a safe. I find, incidentally, that the criminalized children are more competent and rewarding to teach then those who are just angry and oppositional. Criminal propensities are often the sign of a strong will, motivation, self-discipline, and intellectual competence.

Intrinsic in residential treatment is a general perception among the residents that they are at the end of the line. Here are some dismal reflections on the subject.

> I Peaches was on Leake & Watts for two years and 12 days. It's been the worst time of my life. But out of the two years and 12 days I've been here, it has been kind of fun. But usually I'm always upset. There are some residents that I admire a lot. I'd rather not name the residents, because there are too many of them.
>
> Yes, I'm doing good in school until I went to court and found I had to stay here. It was the worst time of my life. I didn't want to stay, but I had to. Yes, I'm going to admit I've been very bad since the day after court. I just changed at once, but there's one thing I learned at that time, that I was bringing it down on myself. No one told me. I just had to learn on my own to know what I was doing to myself. And when I learned things just had to stop at once because I was going down the drain like dirty water. Once people tried to talk, but I just didn't want to listen to no one until I was almost apart. I just had to understand what was happening to me before things get worse.

The sense of "going down the drain like dirty water" is pervasive among the children at an agency. What is generally less pervasive is this girl's inchoate and tenuous resolve to turn things around. She left before we were able to help her, and the last I heard she was back home and expecting a child.

An inevitable consequence of bringing together undersocialized children, whether in an agency or a special education classroom, is that the extremes of behavior that were once deemed antisocial or unacceptable become the norm. When a new resident first comes to the agency, there is generally an initial period of temperate behavior during which the limits are being explored and assessed. Once the measure of things has been taken, the behavior will then slide down to the prevailing norm. I have frequently been confronted by my students' accusatory observation that their behavior has become more wild and disruptive since they have come to Leake & Watts. Here is a piece by a new arrival who is at once appalled by the pervasive bad behavior and yet fails to grasp that his own bad behavior has been the cause of his placement at Leake & Watts.

> Today is a very hot day and I went for a walk because coming to class is so boring that it depresses me so I try to come and try not to get depressed.
>
> There are so many disruptive people in these classes that it is very disturbing because I try to come to class to learn but it is very hard because of those people.
>
> I think I would like it better if I were inside a classroom alone so I could concentrate, but being that it is like that I will have to cope with what is here and try to concentrate anyway.
>
> The school would be a lot better if they would eliminate all the ones that disturb the classes and separate those that want to learn so that I could do my work and show them that I could do well in a community school.

The better students constantly complain about having been placed in such a chaotic setting that the will to learn is thwarted and their education is brought to a stop. The standard special ed answer to this is: "If you knew how to behave yourself, you wouldn't be here." And yet these students are absolutely right. To be in a special education school for the conduct-disordered is to be in a setting where learning is largely preempted by behavior management.

Here is another dispirited meditation on life in placement. There is an unfortunate surface resemblance between life in a residential agency and life in the penal system. A child is often sent to Leake & Watts in response to a specific incident or mishap; the placement is administered through the courts; it is for a set period of time; and continued placement is often assigned by a judge.

> I am a resident at Leake & Watts. In the first place I should be home with my mother. In the second place I should have acted right when I was home. Moreover, I've got to stay here 12 months. Therefore I've got to stay here until I learn my lesson. And yet I shall go home.
>
> But nevertheless I'm still a bad kid. In addition to what the court said, I have to serve at least twelve months. Furthermore I'm lucky I'm not in jail. When I go home I'm going to school and then I'm going to stay in the house until the weekend. But I can do good when I go home and do right.

This piece reveals the many conflicting and unresolved perceptions these children have. The primal fact for every child—and an extremely painful one for these children—is: "In the first place I should be home with my mother." Then, many of these children feel some sense of responsibility for the disruption of their home situation: "I should have acted right when I was home." The one thing they never mention in their writings are the failings of their parents. If there is a parent who is drug addicted or mentally incompetent, this is simply too painful to address. The writer of the above piece is even willing to take on the entire burden of her plight: "I've got to stay here until I learn my lesson. And yet I shall go home." The majority of our children would be sent home immediately if there were a viable home to send them to.

This piece then concludes with a fantasy that will almost certainly never come to pass: "But I can do good when I go home and do right." To deny this vision, however, is to admit that the home life and the parent are hopelessly flawed.

Even more painful than losing a parent is for a child to be rejected by a living parent. To be orphaned is to experience one of the inevitable separations that we all must face at one time or another. To know, however, that the person who gave birth to you is alive and well, cooking meals, darning socks, and going to the movies, all while rejecting you, is to face an incomprehensible affront and loss. Some of the gloomier experts claim in fact that this is a trauma from which there is no full recovery. What words of solace are there for this writer:

> Sometimes I wonder how I am where I am and why I am in a group home. What went wrong at home that my mother

threw me out of the house and said Don't come back? I have no home there no more. I still wonder why. What did I do to deserve this treatment? I wonder what my mother is doing at home right now.

I hate this place called Leake & Watts and the people on it and the staff. That's why I'm trying to get off the campus and go to a group home in the city. There I could live in a better place and have a better life and more money and real friends that are not two faced. Well that concludes my story.

Not only do these children feel the pain of rejection; the pathos is compounded by the fact that they continue to harbor an unfailing love for the parents who have abused and neglected them. It is also tragic to observe that they have a limited ability to form satisfying friendships with their peers. While this writer too yearns for "real friends that are not two-faced," the children at Leake & Watts, having had their capacity to trust others vitiated by their early home life, are unable to derive much satisfaction from any of their relationships.

Those who work with them are faced with two choices. Some willfully choose to ignore the histories and get on with the business at hand. This can ease the task in that one is not thinking of the internal obstructions and can focus on the here and now. The other and often more difficult choice is to look into their lives and then try to move ahead in spite of everything. No matter how one chooses to deal with this, the most significant reality of being with these children is the unfailing presence of pain.

This recollection is exceptional for its vivid and minute detail:

The day my father died was very strange. It seems as if he knew he was going to die. It was a summer day in June. To be specific it was June 20, 1983. My mother was in the bathroom fixing her hair and she was about to take her medicine, as I recall, when the phone rang. I picked it up. It was the hospital telling my mother that he had slipped into a coma and that she should get to the hospital as soon as possible and he was calling her name. As soon as I came out of the bathroom she said, "It's time to call your sisters. Get dressed and let's go say goodbye to Daddy."

A tear came to my eye. I was only eleven years old at the time, but I understood at the time. As soon as we got to the hospital all my understandings left. I wondered what's going on. He promised that he would never leave me and that he would always be there for me.

But what's going on? He doesn't even know who I am. Hours have passed and night was beginning to fall. I went into the room where my father lay. He grabs my hand and said, "I love you and I will never leave you."

My Mom walks into the room and says. "Let's go. We'll be back tomorrow."

As soon as we walked out the nurse said, "Ma'am, may I please speak to you alone?"

"Sure," my mother said.

"Alone," the nurse said.

My Mom walked in with a smile and walked out with a frown and she said, "He's gone." And that's the story of my father's death.

Shortly after the father's death the girl became unmanageable and the mother gave her up for placement. The following poem, typed in this pyramid format, is by the same girl and was addressed to the mother who had only recently expelled her:

```
                  Dear Mother,
              I dedicate this to you.
            My motto is to learn as I
          Live to listen to people
        Who have been through what
      I am going through, take
    Advice even when I don't want
  To. So thanks for all you've
Done for me, even though I've
Messed up during my life, put
You through many trials and tribulations.
I'm sorry for what I've done. I love
You.
```

The children's overwhelming sense of sadness stops me in my tracks again and again. I am lenient with "acting out" behavior, as the alternative is often crushing depression. I find that no matter how hard we try to empathize with these children, the real depth of their pain lies beyond our vision. When I try to introspect about the sources of my own hopes, my will to succeed, and my self-regard, I enter into a regression that takes me back to the earliest stages of my life. And these are the years when these children failed to receive the assurances necessary for the creation of a viable adult.

These writings by my students convey something of the sadness and frustration that envelop anyone who works with them. The day creeps by at an exasperatingly slow pace, and I find that I am looking at the clock every ten minutes. The day finally does come to an end and the children do not really want to leave school, as they have no place to go where they will receive as much attention. When the final bell rings at 3:00 P.M. I am usually in conversation with a student, and I am as loathe to leave as he is. By 3:15 I leave the building and climb back up the hill to the crest behind the administration building. At this point I have neither the energy nor the sentiment to look back down at the school and the river. I am asking myself how I am going to get through the next day.

2

High Spirits and Bad Behavior

The ways in which I find my work stimulating and rewarding, devastating and exhausting, all have to do with oppositional behavior. There is a type of person who goes into this work—and I recognize myself as fitting this category—who was himself once a prankster, a troublemaker, and a teacher-baiter. Such staff have the advantage of finding the children's behavior familiar and engaging, even when their position forces them to reprimand and discipline. The largest part of my time is spent in dealing with evasions, affronts, and contentiousness—most of which I find amusing even while trying to bring them under control.

Bad behavior falls into a few very basic categories: fighting, oppositional attitude, theft, and verbal abuse. Today's pranks and mischief are little different from what the children of Leake & Watts were doing 150 years ago. Unfortunately, these behaviors, if pursued with sufficient persistence, will force a child out of the mainstream of schooling and family life. Some of the vignettes presented may seem benign and harmless, and yet they are all indicative of failed socialization.

23

When we read the newspaper aloud in class and there is a story about the Pope, I want my students to learn that he resides in the Vatican. I tell them that the Vatican is the home of the Pope and that a Vatican spokesman is someone who speaks for the Catholic Church. The next day I ask the class who lives in the Vatican, and the answer comes back, "Your mother!"

This is of course unacceptable and, in my task to educate and socialize, I would be remiss to let it go. I cannot really bring myself to put on a grave demeanor and explain that such inappropriate language will prevent my students from obtaining satisfactory employment and desirable social access in later life. In this instance I explain to the student with mock gravity that my mother has passed on, that she had never been to Rome, and that anyway there was no room for her at the Vatican.

This became a recurring theme, as the Pope was visiting the United States and there was daily coverage. I would laboriously ask who aside from my mother lived in the Vatican, and after some further variations on the theme of my mother in improbable roles, this wisecrack was put to rest.

There was a sequel several months later when the Pope was once again in the paper and a Vatican spokesman was quoted. I again asked the class who lived in the Vatican, and the same student raised her hand and said with a smirk, "Mr. Howe's mother," she paused, "and the Pope."

For those who are willing to take it lightly, conduct disorder can be amusing and not necessarily destructive to pedagogic ends. In order to carry on I must take liberties with propriety and give my students latitude. To be sharp and abrupt with the purely mischievous aspect of conduct disorder is to exhaust my energies and provoke the child into obstinacy.

It took me about a year to learn to employ a light and oblique style of dealing with the children. It is a style that is pervasive throughout the agency and it creates an aura of levity that allows much of the children's pain and anger to slip by unnoticed.

Along with the abusive language, there is a lot of horseplay that verges on a full-fledged fight, but seldom becomes one. It is chiefly the male students who engage in this: they are constantly staging mock-threatening situations in which both partners take their stand and then allow one another to back down with dignity. They love to involve the staff in these situations, and it is often hard to resist.

In a typical instance a student who is cutting his regular class will burst into my room and refuse to leave when I ask him to do so. There then follows a rather formulaic pursuit across the room and behind my desk. The student will finally let me catch him and forcibly escort him from the room, provided that I am begging him all the while not to hurt me.

In another version he will stand off in a combative pose and announce, "Man, I'm going to wax you, Howe."

I then close the distance, full of determination, and ask, "What do you want to wax an old man for? The jails are full of teacher-bashers." He will then allow me to escort him from the room.

To meet opposition with amused indulgence is to blunt the anger behind it. When I do this I try not to lose sight of my goal—whether it is removing someone from my room or getting a student to start working. Many of them would be happy to spend the entire day in lighthearted roughhousing with me, and as the years pass, I find less and less reason to object.

The most pervasive manifestation of dissocial conduct is an unremitting attitude of opposition. These children will not do what they are told to do. Beyond this, they will go out of their way to do things they know they are not supposed to do. And when disciplined, they will respond with anger—usually in the form of foul and abusive language, but sometimes with physical violence.

More often oppositional behavior is entertaining—such kids have high-level ability with insult and invective. When, for example, one of my students asks leave to go to the bathroom, another will remark, "He doesn't have to go to the bathroom. He just wants to jerk off again." When someone asks me for a pencil, another student will say, "Your illiterate ass doesn't even know how to read. What are you going to do with a pencil?" When a student from another class appears at the window in my door to ask a question, one of my students will exclaim, "Get your ugly face back to your class. No dogs allowed here."

Of the many manifestations of opposition, the one that affects me most as a teacher is the children's resistance to being educated. Many of their referrals originate with schools, since school is the place that makes the most consistent demands for conformity. Most of my students have stories about being called to the principal's office at their former school, first alone and then with their parents, to account for acts of abuse, violence, vandalism, and disobedience.

As a result, a child is taken out of the mainline of instruction and placed in special education classes. This means that they associate all schooling with the attempt to control their behavior. After several years of this they hate school and have academic skills that can lag five or six years behind the norm.

Perhaps their most frequent complaint about their school work is that "it's boring." By the time they are 15 there is a vicious cycle of boredom, leading to resistance, to bad behavior, and finally to a low level of academic performance. The substance of their behaviors day in day out are refusal to do work, frequent and extended visits to the bathroom, absurd and fictitious "emergencies" that require departure from class, altercations with classmates, temper tantrums, and sleeping.

A typical dodge is the sudden need to take care of urgent business. A student will leap up from her desk and exclaim, "I have to see my social worker. Give me a pass to the office." When I ask why, I find that the student wants to know what time she will be allowed to leave the grounds for a home pass five days hence. I try to take at least a token stand against episodes of this sort, as the issue is being able to concentrate on one thing—in this case, school work—and imposing some sense of progress and priorities on the flow of the day.

Another popular dodge is the sudden and insurmountable aversion to one's work. When I ask a student to read aloud to me from a book she has been using for the last several weeks, she will announce angrily, "I hate this book. It's stupid. I want a different book." This too is a battle worth fighting, as these children have become so accustomed to fragmentation and discontinuity that a two-hour movie or a 50-page book will stretch their attention span to its limit. I find, however, that when I hold the line in such matters, my students will come to view a book they have read from end to end as a prized trophy.

Then there are the tricks intended to test a teacher's patience and ability to deal with dawdling. A student will announce, "I can't do my work without a pencil. What do you want me to write with, my finger?" I will then give him a pencil, and he will say, "No, not a short one. Give me a new one or I'm not working."

In a similar but more disruptive vein, a student will come in late, walk up to a student who is at work, and announce, "Get out of my desk. That is my seat." When I finally convince the late student that he has lost his right to his desk by arriving late, he will shove his work onto the floor and announce, "I'm not working. I don't like this desk. It's too hard."

These are the little scenes that engage my energy throughout the day—more so than actual teaching, and I try to meet them with indirection. To the student who says that his friend has gone to the bathroom to jerk off, I will say, "Don't worry. As soon as he comes back you can go." To the student who wants a new pencil, one can say, "I'll give you a new pencil—right across the back of the head." To the student who finds her book boring I will say, "I was born to bore. I once had a student die of boredom in my classroom." Such answers have the effect of turning a possible confrontation into something lighthearted. And although such a response does not put an end to this kind of opposition, in time it does soften the aggressive intent.

An important outlet for the hostility and anger within these kids is a never-ending torrent of abuse and invective. They employ incredibly cruel and abusive language all the time. No physical anomaly will escape their taunts. If a resident is exceptionally dark skinned, he will be called a "black baboon" by his peers. Someone with unusually thick lips will be warned not to catch them in the door on the way out of the room. If a resident has been abandoned by his or her entire family, someone will say, "You're so disgusting, your parents don't even want you home on Christmas." Someone with an overbite is a "snaggle-toothed hyena," while someone with a swayback and rounded rear end will be called "Bubble Butt." If a resident requires medication to control psychosis, he will be called a "Thorazine zombie." If a resident has dyslexia and is learning-disabled, his classmates will ask him to spell "cat" and "dog" and he will be taunted no matter what the answer.

The style of opposition and acting out varies somewhat between the boys and the girls. The male response to authority and supervision tends to be evasion and horseplay, while the girls are more apt to be intransigent and resistant. When the male playfulness runs out of control, it manifests itself as a high level of mischief, and when the evasiveness runs out of control, the boy will simply drop out of the picture. This can take the form of going out of program, or even drug abuse.

Whichever of these two it happens to be, the staff who work with the males are spared the full force of their pain and anger. On occasion a male resident will take the level of horseplay to a point where he must be forcibly removed. The preferred mode, however, (and one spends a great deal of time at this) is an endless game of cat and mouse. Here I am at work with Jamal F., a plump and amiable 14-year-old from Brooklyn.

"Do your work. The book is open to the page."

"I already did this yesterday. Anyway, it is stupid."

"The work you did yesterday is in a different book. And in fact you did not do anything yesterday. You were out of the program. Here is a pencil. I don't want a word from you until you finish the page."

Ten seconds pass.

"You never showed me how to do this."

"Don't even try it. You're reducing fractions, just like last year with Miss Kelly."

"O yeah, that stupid shit."

Many of the boys are perfectly happy to go on like this for an entire period. Such an exchange is not especially exhausting for the teacher, and for the student it is an amusing way to kill an afternoon. Usually the game is played out to some mutually understood point of depletion and the boy will either do a modicum of work, gaze out the window, or sleep.

Here is Barbara G., an extremely resistant and foul-spoken 15-year-old from the Bronx who was in my class two years ago. She will come into the room with the wrath of God on her brow, and I will venture a very tentative "Good morning."

She will drop into her desk without looking up and grumble, "Shut the fuck up."

Obviously I should intrude as little as possible, and when the period gets under way I will pass out folders, coming to her desk last in sequence. She hurls the folder on the floor, says, "Don't give me that fucking shit," and then buries her head in her arms.

At this point I can choose between saying, "I will not have this language in my room. Please get up and leave." Or I can let her fume in silence for the rest of the period.

Since there really is no place other than the school for the overflow of these feelings, I will keep Barbara in class as long as she does not become a menace. Incidentally, by the end of two years, Barbara had simply cussed herself out and had become reasonably temperate with her language and anger. Last June I had the pleasure of watching her receive her high school diploma from one of the community schools in Yonkers.

What is often difficult to anticipate, both for the staff and the children, is the point at which playful banter or moody resistance can erupt into hard aggression. When I endeavor to curtail this kind of abusive talk, the standard response is, "We're just playing." The dark side comes when the verbal abuse escalates into slap-fighting which in turn becomes a full-fledged battle requiring staff intervention. As a teacher with a professional commitment to the safety of these children I must constantly discern the thin line that separates harmless play from serious aggression.

The most hazardous form of dissocial behavior is fighting. The penchant for fighting arises from two sources. Having received little nurture, these children have a naturally hostile and aggressive attitude toward others. In addition to the anger and aggression, many have an explosive temper over which they have no control. It is essential for those working with them to be able to sense the moment when an incident that started with taunts and insults threatens to be resolved with a kitchen knife or a hammer.

Grave violence can be provoked in the most trifling and innocuous circumstances. When I first came to Leake & Watts there was an apparently genial and massively built young man of 15. He was in several of my classes and I found him to be generally agreeable and eager to please. I later learned that the agency was waiting for him to turn 16 so they could press charges for assault and have him removed to a more restrictive facility. It turned out that he had ripped every thread of clothing off the girl next to him in class. A taunting conversation had escalated, she had jabbed him in the forehead with the tip of a pencil, and he went wild. On another occasion he struck a student full force on the arm with a golf club, snapping the bone clean through. And on yet another occasion he had swatted a resident across the back with the thick end of a pool cue, breaking the cue in the process.

This was an exceptionally violent child, and such events are atypical. Generally the residents prefer to avoid a violent physical confrontation, but they are very happy to bring their altercations to the brink of violence. When things are at the brink, their sense of reality and self-control is so tenuous that anything can happen. A student in my class hurled a pair of scissors at another resident in response to a cruel remark. On another occasion a male student burst into my class and made a sexually provocative remark to one of the girls. I saw the look of desperate anger in her face soon enough to prevent her from whacking him with the sewing machine she was working at. She had already lifted it over her head and was advancing toward him.

Although many of these acts of aggression are done with little manifest intent of doing serious harm, a resident will get unlucky every now and then and score a direct hit. A couple of residents got into an argument over a piece of clothing. Neither of them impressed me at the time as being particularly violent. Tara B. had reproached Yvonne J. for taking a blouse from her. The tempers started to heat up and suddenly Yvonne seized a bottle of ketchup and hurled it at Tara. Tara ended up in the hospital with stitches and a concussion, while Yvonne was taken down to the local police precinct and booked for assault. Both the children involved in this incident were assigned to my home room, and it was feared that one of them would have to be removed from the school program to prevent further violence. By the end of a week, however, they were chatting and joking together as though nothing had ever happened.

There are regular incidents of this sort involving broom handles and even fire extinguishers—whatever might be at hand when tempers explode. A violent temper is of course a great deal more dangerous and unmanageable than verbal abuse. In fact, it can happen that a child who has abandoned verbal abuse or uses it only in a lighthearted way is still capable of physical violence. The short-term anger that led to the sharp language may have subsided due to overuse or depletion, while the underlying tendency to menacing behavior lies deeper and is not as susceptible to change. Children who have made great progress in day-to-day socialization will suddenly and unexpectedly inflict such violence on another resident or staff member that charges are pressed and the police are called in.

One resident, Alberto, is extremely popular with all the staff because he is so tractable and obliging. He rarely creates any difficulty for anyone and is always eager to please. If, however, he loses his temper, nothing will bring him under control short of a full-scale restraint procedure involving two to four adults. It will take no more than a minor affront from another resident to precipitate such an outburst, and this normally docile young man will employ on all who come into his path the full range of karate kicks and body slamming techniques now in favor for street fighting. On a couple of occasions he has gone after other residents and I have rather foolishly taken it upon myself to get in his way. He weighs about 100 pounds more than I do and was able to brush me aside with a casual swing of his arm. Once the incident was over, however, and his temper had simmered down, he came to me with great solicitude to ask if I had been hurt. It was as though the episode had involved an entirely different person.

Like so many dissocial children, Alberto had endured incalculable pain and abuse during his formative years. Just because he had spent a couple of years in the relatively supportive environment of a residential agency, he was not yet ready to forgive his past and control his impulsiveness.

It is recognized by all—including the children—that they do not really want to get hurt, so if they must provoke a fight, they will choose the most protective environment—which is the school. Recently, I heard two girls arguing menacingly in the hall. As I approached them and took a position more or less between them, they raised their voices and became more threatening toward one another. At this point another staff member approached, and once he was standing right next to one of the girls, she lunged at the other. We were able to separate them before they were able to land a blow and as we pulled them apart, they exchanged vows of major violence at their next meeting.

After it was over, it occurred to me that had I not approached them, the exchange probably never would have gone beyond verbal threats. What, if anything was gained by my approaching them and then breaking up their fight? It could be argued that they were given an opportunity to give harmless expression to powerful feelings that could have erupted later on in a more destructive manner. It could also be argued that they were putting the school to the test as a safe and caring place, and we were not found wanting. It is interesting to note that the children especially respect and appreciate an adult who will step in to break up a fight when there is a chance of getting hurt. Conversely, a fight will occasionally break out in the presence of a staff member who then does not step in. At such times it becomes painfully clear how much they count on us, as they never fail to express their rage at an adult who will not step into the middle of a fight.

If the staff does intervene quickly, if no serious injuries are inflicted, and if the combatants are counseled in an emphatic but supportive manner, then some small progress is made toward controlling their combative tendencies.

When it comes to fighting and intemperate behavior, I find that the majority of the seasoned pros in this field prefer the boys to the girls. The girls are held to be more tempestuous, more ungoverned, and less amenable to staff supervision. The difference in their respective behaviors lies, I believe, in the latitude our culture allows a male for his emotional life. The model of male behavior is the rigid jaw and the unmoist eye. What does this mean for a male adolescent who has endured a high level of pain? What it means, at least with the males I see, is a playful and evasive way of dealing with experience. The girls, on the other hand, do not hesitate to make full disclosure of the intensity of their feelings. When the girls get into a fight, it can be truly disquieting. The one thing all the staff dreads is breaking up a fight between girls. They will go after one another with a murderous rage and are happy to employ the nearest object, blunt or sharp, that comes to hand.

In a typical incident, two girls in my class got into an altercation over who had the first claim to a certain desk. Joan J. was considerably larger than Nicole F., so Nicole backed down, saying under her breath, "Your mother." Nicole was unaware of the fact that Joan's mother had recently passed on and that she had just spoken the unspeakable. Joan went after her with her finger nails, leaving long bleeding scratch marks along Nicole's neck. In an attempt to defend herself, Nicole pulled at Joan's blouse. Suddenly Joan was without blouse or brassiere still tearing at Nicole's flesh. They went at each other with a crazed violence that took two robust males to subdue.

The boys tend to go "straight up," which means they take a pugilist stance and exchange blows. These fights are more often an issue of honor and insult rather than an eruption of blind rage. I find that if I step into the midst of most fist fights, the combatants will usually lower their fists and resort to taunts. Since the boys are stronger, hit harder, and are more expert fighters, they are generally grateful for adult intervention before someone gets hurt.

A classic manifestation of dissocial behavior is stealing. Where there has been sound nurture, the child will refrain from stealing out of the desire to please the parent—assuming the parent opposes stealing. If the child then continues to refrain from stealing and receives approval, he will internalize the parent's rejection of stealing. Such a child is then on the way to having a conscience with a capacity for guilt and remorse.

It is curious to observe the ways in which the children will

steal. Although there are occasional acts of planned and clandes-
tine theft where the prize is considerable, the norm consists of
trifling and overt acts of grabbing, snatching, and forceful appro-
priation. When it comes to major larceny, there have been only a
handful of incidents in the last three years. On one occasion a
couple of students broke into the school store and took a bunch of
candy bars and comic books. On another occasion two of them
drove off with an agency van after loading on it the recreation
department safe. Since they could not open the safe, they dumped
it in the river, and then they abandoned the van about ten miles
from the agency. They had embarked on a large-scale operation
that exceeded their ability to think out the problems and plan
ahead.

Petty theft, on the other hand, is rife. Although stealing
suggests a certain degree of social chaos, a code in fact governs
most of the stealing that takes place. Typically, one child will
simply take something from a weaker child, especially one whom
he or she does not happen to like. This can be as overt as taking
food from a person's plate, or snitching an article of clothing and
then flaunting it around the grounds—an act of naked aggression
supported by superior strength.

A further refinement in the code of theft is the distinction
between stealing as an act of aggression and stealing because something has been left unguarded. Anyone who is negligent will be
stolen from, and it has happened to me. A typical instance occurred when I had left the cabinet in my classroom open and
turned my back to take care of some papers on my desk. I was aware
of a student entering the room and perusing the contents of my
cabinet. After about 30 seconds he walked out, and that afternoon
I noticed that a baseball was missing. I confronted him directly,
asking, "Where is my baseball?"

He looked me over with cool amusement and said, "It is in my
cottage."

"I would like it back."

"I'll bet you would. That's too bad." This was the note on
which the matter was left to rest.

Occasionally thereafter I would ask, "How about my baseball?"

And he would respond with a smirk, "How about it?"

"How about bringing it back?"

"It's in my cottage. Why don't you come up and try to get it?"

By now it had become a game, but it was a game I had lost because I had been inattentive and hence forfeited my right to the ball.

On other occasions I have had the pockets of my jacket emptied. Since I know that an unattended jacket is fair game, I leave only chalk and pencils in the pockets. If they are stolen, it is because I am being negligent, and the same would happen to my wallet if I were to leave it in my jacket unattended.

In large matters, however, many of these students will return trust with probity and decency. I keep several hundred dollars worth of my own camera equipment in the school and have on occasion lent it out overnight and even over the weekend to the students. Although they never tire of teasing me about how much money they could get for my equipment on the street, they have so far done nothing about it. I believe that they appreciate the trust and will do what they can to live up to my expectations.

An interesting test in which my students seldom let me down is lending out objects overnight. My students know that I own tapes of some of the rap groups, and they are constantly after me to let them "hold" a tape—which basically means to let them keep it for an indeterminate period of time. In most instances I get the tape back the moment I ask for it. There have, however, been a couple of occasions when I have been told, "My brother has it in Brooklyn," or "Someone stole it from my cottage." This is a dodge and it means, "Don't ask about it because you are not getting it back."

We are not able to eliminate stealing, but we generally contain it within limits. That is to say, the stronger children will steal regularly from the weaker ones, and on occasion there will be a major act of larceny. The matter can get out of hand when the children enter a store where a lot of merchandise is out on display—say, a supermarket or a dime store. One resident was famous for being able to stuff his coat with enough food to feed half a dozen people. He would go into a deli or small market—one without a checkout position at the door—and circle the freezer, the chips and cookies, and the soda chiller. He would then depart absent-mindedly with his coat bulging. I have a student in my present class who went down to Macy's over the winter recess with an empty knapsack and returned with his entire spring wardrobe on his back.

For many of the children the desirable objects they see out on display are no different from the baseball in my cabinet. If someone is not paying attention, he is a fool and his goods are up for grabs. This kind of minor pilfering is rife and, for those who do not break the habit, there is the likelihood of trouble later in life. Although most of them learn how to adapt to the agency and stay out of trouble, they do not come to terms with the impulses that cause them to steal in the first place. When I first came to Leake & Watts, I offered a course on ethics and moral choices. For reasons to be discussed shortly, it was a washout.

Another pervasive form of dissocial behavior is truancy. In its broadest sense this simply means failing to be where one is supposed to be. Prior to placement most of the residents at Leake & Watts had a history of truancy in the sense that they were chronically absent from school, or stayed away from home for extended periods of time.

This type of misconduct arises out of a general disregard for rules. The adolescent who is truant from school grows up to be the adult who is chronically absent from work. It is a habit of defiance and noncompliance that finds the expectations of society repressive and irrelevant.

The children think little of skipping school or going AWOL to return to their old neighborhoods. They will make selective decisions as to which classes they will attend and which they will cut. They will "go out of program" entirely, which often consists in leaving the grounds and hanging out downtown.

On the one hand, the agency tries to make the children answerable for their obligations; on the other hand, the school staff and house parents will wink at a minor infraction rather than set off the pernicious cycle of scolding and punishment that is often followed by explosive anger and even more egregious truancy.

One of the debilitating features of working with the children is their apparent inability to respond to discipline. Dereliction and punishment have occurred in their lives in an endless succession. When I scold or threaten a child, a frequent response is, "What can you do me?" This means that whatever punishment I may have in mind, he has experienced worse in the past and is prepared to do so again in the future.

I have a very intelligent student this year, Ned M., whose father is in prison. He is totally inured to the threat of punishment, as he knows that the worst anyone can do to him is what has happened to his father. To deter a child like this from misconduct requires not a stronger, but a different disciplinary medicine.

And yet despite the tragic implications, I generally feel behind all the high spirits and bad behavior an exuberant sense of play and defiance. We create social norms with the expectation that there is going to be someone out there to break them. When I am in the corridors with throngs of children who should be in class, but are play-fighting, laughing, and cursing, I feel that I am in attendance at the ongoing saturnalia—the titanic belch at a formal dinner—that enforces the necessity of all rules and conventions.

3

The Undersocialized Child

The impediment most likely to prevent the children of Leake & Watts from becoming competent adults is their oppositional and antisocial behavior. Seen in this light, bad behavior is a crippling condition that can be as debilitating as a physical ailment. Over the years there have been many different terms employed to describe the child who is either unmanageable, criminally inclined, or both. What was called juvenile delinquency 30 years ago is now the Conduct Disorder of Adolescence. August Aichhorn, a professional educator and the definitive writer on the subject in the 1920s, used the more poetic phrase "Wayward Youth" to describe the adolescents who are at odds with society and with their elders. Although the terminology has changed, the underlying cause and the manifestation are clear and consistent. To work with such children is never gratifying in the conventional sense of the term, for this is not a matter of setting goals, seeing them come to timely fruition, and then receiving heartfelt thanks for one's exertions.

When I first started teaching the children at Leake & Watts, I immediately became aware of two things. First, I liked the job;

and second, I was expending more energy during the day than I was recovering at night and over the weekends. If I become personally engaged in their lives and problems—and it is hard not to—the magnitude of my task and the tiny increments of progress try the spirit and exhaust my energies. The conflict of being both stimulated and depleted by this work is experienced by many. Some eventually distance themselves from the children and retreat into administration, paperwork, or the many activities that assess the problem rather than treat it. Others leave the field entirely, feeling that they have served their tour of duty. Still others stay on to return the children's anger with their own.

And yet the fact remains that the people who go into this kind of work are generally high-minded, idealistic, and in search of a cause in which to lose themselves. There are of course the occasional bullies and browbeaters, but this is the exception rather than the rule. Even for the best and most generous-hearted, however, there comes a point at which it is difficult to rise above the opposition, anger, and chaos. As a detached professional, one knows that the anger is not to be taken personally, and yet it is hard to stifle a purely elemental response to so much raw opposition.

As long as I have been at Leake & Watts, my resilience in dealing with the children has been tenuous and subject to collapse. Once I started to familiarize myself with the psychoanalytical literature on the early development of the dissocial child, the job became more coherent and hence somewhat more tolerable. After a while I was able to frame the problem in precise and humane terminology that explained bad behavior as the result of insufficient love during the first five years of life. This means that the primary task of the child care worker is to nurture the child with "compensatory love." The problems of the children—poor self-esteem, no impulse control, aggressive behavior, an undeveloped moral code—can be traced in great measure to a lack of loving attention during the early years of life.

The seminal figure in the treatment of oppositional children is August Aichhorn, who ran a home for difficult children outside Vienna in the 1920s. Aichhorn studied psychoanalysis, became a protégé of Freud, and applied psychoanalytic concepts of early development to the problems of antisocial behavior. His classic study, *Verwahrloste Jugend*, first published in 1925, was translated into English 10 years later as *Wayward Youth*. Over the next 25 years his insights were elaborated by others with psychoanalytic training, including such notables as Anna Freud and Kate Friedlander, whose work with children who had been displaced by World War II led to her book, *The Psychoanalytical Approach to Juvenile Delinquency.*

Both Aichhorn and Friedlander posited that delinquent behavior was the result of irregular nurture during the first five years of life, and they both blamed the irregular nurture on wartime conditions. The father has been out of the home, and the mother may have been separated from her children because of evacuation procedures. The histories of the children at Leake & Watts, however, suggest circumstances that have been no less chaotic than was the case in Austria and England in time of war. I am referring specifically to the absence of a father, to separation from the mother, to constantly changing caretakers, to overcrowding, and material deprivation.

This view of the dissocial child asserts that antisocial behavior results from the failure of an infant to experience reliable and consistent satisfaction of bodily and emotional needs. The socialization of every human being consists in suppressing instinctive and libidinal needs in favor of considerations that embrace a larger circle of humanity. The world of the infant, like that of the animal, revolves around food, shelter, sleep, and other similar, purely physical needs. The first step in the circle of expanding awareness comes when the infant forms a relationship with the mother or primary caretaker responsible for meeting appetitive needs. If care has been loving, reliable, and consistent, then this first relationship with the mother will foster trust and willingness to postpone gratification. The willingness to postpone gratification is the first all-important step toward the capacity to subordinate one's own needs to the requirements of others. The infant who does not receive satisfactory instinctive gratification during the first year of life will be more inclined to enter the second and third years with an angry and aggressive view of the world. Such an infant will have a tendency toward fits of temper and extended crying.

Not having formed a loving bond with the parent, the child is not prepared to postpone gratification. Thus, not only is the infant angry and aggressive, he also has little ability to accommodate his instinctive needs to the wishes of others. The infant who has not learned to trust the mother to meet his needs fails to develop the will and courage to emerge from the narrow world of instinctual gratification to the socialized world of love and trust. Conversely, the child who has learned to rely on the mother's love will be more inclined to accept a regular feeding schedule, will be more amenable to bathroom training, and will be more tolerant of siblings.

The next developmental step, commencing around the age of three, is when the child acquires the first elements of moral restraint. Impelled by feelings of love and trust, the child will begin to emulate and internalize the parent's code of conduct. If, however, the parent fails to provide consistent love and nurture, the child feels little need to win the parent's approval or to emulate the parent's mode of conduct. The child will give little heed or credence to such social niceties as, "You should not steal," or "Don't hit other children," or "It is nice to share." The usual consequence of ungratifying and inconsistent nurture is that the child reaches the age of five dominated by instincts, aggressive toward others, and lacking the moral constraints that will ensure a harmonious adaptation to the world at large.

This means that by the age of five the child who has had poor nurture will have an inclination toward a bad temper, to acts of hostility and aggression, and a poorly developed sense of remorse and moral direction. This describes the basic problem of the children who come to Leake & Watts, and it is the same problem that August Aichhorn was dealing with 60 years ago.

The seeds of behavior disorder are planted during the first years of life, and much of the clinical literature takes a dim view of the ability of these children to respond to any kind of treatment. The theory of deprivation holds that there has been an irreplaceable omission in their earliest development because they were deprived of loving care at the very beginning of their life. This theory is based on the work of the Austrian naturalist Konrad Lorenz. From his observation of greylag geese he learned that if at the moment of hatching there is a parent figure to respond to their "lost piping" sound, the babies will follow the parent around and look to it for protection. If, however, there is no parent figure—be it human, mechanical, or goose—the gosling will not develop the capacity to follow the parent and seek nurture. Thus the ability to form a bond is not so much a learned behavior as it is a response that is released by the parent's initial solicitude.

Lorenz postulates, and many psychoanalysts and psychologists agree, that one of the essential experiences in the life of a higher animal is forming an immediate bond with the parent figure. Lacking this experience, the animal—whether goose or human—fails to receive the "imprint" that will enable this particular kind of behavior. And if this is so, then it is possible for a person to come to adolescence or even adulthood with a limited ability to make a significant connection with others.

The deprivation theory is both highly suggestive and highly pessimistic. It is convincing in that the students at Leake & Watts do present layers upon layers of resistance to the adults who want to love and care for them. And yet this kind of work must be supported by a humane belief that love and concern can overpower anger and indifference. It also helps to believe that people are more adaptable than greylag geese. Where animals may require "imprinting" as a quick and efficient device for survival, the hope is that children can process a broader range of experience and come up with more resourceful responses.

In this regard working with dissocial children is "redemptive" in the literal sense of the word "redeem"—meaning "to buy back." These children have received an insufficient portion of loving attention and, as a result, have drifted beyond the norms of acceptable behavior. One hopes that, while they are in placement, an enlarged portion of loving attention may buy back some of the loss. To the extent that residential treatment is not able to make good on the loss, however, the work is more custodial than curative.

One can gather at least an inkling of the early deprivation by looking at individual case histories. Although the records are often vague and fragmentary, they provide a coherent and consistent picture of lives gone wrong. The individual histories of the children of Leake & Watts are protected by stringent state and city laws of privacy, as well as by the scrupulous policies observed by that private agency. Their experiences have many salient features in common, however, and the following two composite histories are representative.

The most common story at Leake & Watts is the one told by Richard Wright in his autobiography, *Black Boy*: Extreme poverty and crushing racism in the rural South forced American blacks to migrate to Northern cities in search of employment and equal opportunity. Then Claude Brown's *Manchild in the Promised Land* tells how inner-city blacks, newly arrived from farms, experienced the chaos and socioeconomic isolation that produced the generation now residing at Leake & Watts. What we are dealing with is the culmination of two or three generations of American blacks looking for a viable life in a major city, and not finding it.

The children of Leake & Watts are all referred from within New York City and have all experienced the same street life. Ruth's case, a composite of several actual histories, is representative of what is happening to these children:

> Ruth was born of a sixteen-year-old mother in North Carolina. The mother was a junior in high school at the time and never told Ruth anything about the identity of her father.
>
> Ruth was born in December and moved in with her grandmother so that her mother could finish out the school year. At the end of the school year Ruth's mother decided to quit school and move north to Brooklyn, so that Ruth's aunt (the mother's older sister) could take care of her while the mother went to beauty culture school. The aunt already had children of her own whom Ruth came to view as her own siblings.
>
> During Ruth's first year in New York, her mother married and moved out of the house. Since the mother's husband was apparently unwilling to have Ruth in the house, Ruth continued to live with her aunt.
>
> Ruth stayed with the aunt until she was almost four. At this time the aunt's occasional problem with drug addiction went out of control and Ruth was no longer able to stay with her. Ruth was found to be suffering from malnutrition at the time.
>
> The natural mother had a new family with her husband and was unable or unwilling to take Ruth in. At the age of four Ruth was sent back to North Carolina to live with the grandmother. Apparently, there was a prolonged period— about ten years—during which Ruth lived with the grandmother, attended school regularly, and did well. When Ruth was 13, however, the grandmother developed crippling arthritis and both Ruth and the grandmother went back to Brooklyn to live with the natural mother in a two bedroom apartment. Ruth's mother had now divorced her husband, but had two children by him.
>
> The grandmother's condition worsened rapidly and she died in less than a year. Ruth immediately became truant from school, started having violent fights with her younger siblings, and would stay away from home for as much as a week at a time. The mother found that she could not handle Ruth and had her placed in foster care.

Ruth's story represents a Leake & Watts norm. The following features are likely to precipitate behavior disorder:

The child did not have the benefit of the mother's care during the first six months of life. This means that the all-important initial experience of instinctual satisfaction had not taken place at the hands of the mother, and the bonds arising from this relationship were six months in arrears from the beginning. Of course, had the grandmother continued to be the primary caretaker, this would not have been critical, as good nurture is good nurture, irrespective of who is providing it.

This scenario of early deprivation occurs again and again with slight variations. The natural mother will be drug-addicted, will have psychiatric problems, will abandon the child at birth. From then on there will be a makeshift sequence of temporary caretakers, and with that the first seed of flawed development is planted.

The child was never in an intact home with both a father and mother available. Then in Ruth's case there was a change in primary caretakers. The permanence of a constant loving presence, whether it is the mother, the grandmother, an aunt, or even a neighbor, is all-important to the development of the infant's self-esteem, impulse control, and ability to accommodate the wishes of others. There is nothing like working with these children to impress upon one the gravity of being a parent and the drastic results of neglectful parenting.

Ruth was rejected by her mother. To have known one's mother and then be rejected by her is a worse trauma than never to have known her at all. There are numerous instances where lack of money, overcrowding, the arrival of a boyfriend or new husband, or difficult behavior will prompt a mother to put up a child for placement. In extreme instances there are girls who have been sexually abused by their mother's lover only to have the mother reject the child and keep the man.

Many of the young mothers of these children find themselves in situations that are so desperate and chaotic that they are forced to fall back on the older generation—typically the grandmother—to keep things going. If the grandmother has become the primary caretaker and then passes away at a critical time of life for the child, the result can be a vehement and unexpected eruption of dissocial behavior. Aichhorn employs the term "latent delinquency" to describe the condition of a child who has been emotionally deprived but waits to manifest antisocial behavior until some much later experience precipitates it.

Under healthy conditions, a child between the age of three and five will start to deal successfully with experiences that require moral discernment. Defective moral development can arise from two sources. In the more improbable instance there is the child who has a strong bond with a morally unsound parent—say, a child who is raised by kind and loving thieves. In this case the child tries to gratify the parents by internalizing their code. The more typical case is of the child who has a tenuous bond with a morally sound parent. Then the child will harbor so much resentment toward the parent that he is unwilling to submit to the inconvenience and self-control required for moral conduct. Thus the approval of the parent is not a sufficient force to induce a child to forbear from stealing or hitting smaller children.

Here is another representative history that illustrates an entirely different set of deprivations:

> Paul's mother and father were living together when he was born, and he was the fourth child. When Paul was 18 months old his mother needed psychiatric hospitalization. The three elder siblings went with the father, who had moved in with another woman shortly before the mother's breakdown.
>
> Paul was sent to live with his maternal grandmother, who also had a history of psychiatric hospitalization. Paul's mother was one of eight children the grandmother had borne, each by a different father. The grandmother had in fact had so much difficulty that Paul's mother had been in foster care.
>
> Paul resided with the grandmother until he was ten. His mother was in and out of the picture, but was apparently too disabled by her psychiatric difficulties to take a significant part in his rearing. The grandmother's competence to deal with Paul was also called into question on several occasions. There were reports from his first grade teacher that he had appeared in school with what appeared to be cigarette burns on his legs. A social worker was called in but the findings were inconclusive.
>
> By the time Paul was in third grade, he was in special ed classes. He was said to be oppositional, hyperactive, constantly taunting his fellow students, and explosive. He has been in special ed classes ever since.
>
> When Paul was twelve his grandmother's behavior became

so erratic that she had to move out of the home, and he never saw her again.

At this time the natural mother happened to be in the home and tried to resume her parental role. Meanwhile, there were repeated reports from school about Paul's fighting and temper tantrums. He finally threw a desk at another student, giving him a concussion. At this point Social Services for Children intervened to remove Paul from school and from his mother's care. He was placed in a group home.

He was in the group home for a year, during which time there were further violent episodes. From the group home he was referred to Leake & Watts. He has a full-scale IQ of 72 and displays an extreme aversion to any form of schooling.

The problem in Paul's case is both medical and social. At any given time 10 to 15 percent of our residents come from a home that has been beset by a medical problem such as mental illness, diabetes, retardation, or tuberculosis. These difficulties can of course also lead to deprivation and flawed personality development.

The undesirable behavior that results from defective nurture will then be evident by the time a child enters school. The child will be placed in a special education class and the problem of bad behavior is compounded by the problem of regressed academic skills, for the longer a child stays in special education classes for disturbed students, the more grave the academic deficits will be.

At the time of this writing, more than three-quarters of the children in the Leake & Watts High School are functioning at a sixth-grade level or less. A significant factor is the many years of troubled schooling in a classroom where behavior management took precedence over education. This means that a child whose conversation, alertness, and responses all bespeak average or above average native intelligence can end up with an IQ in the range of between 70 and 80 by the age of 16. This has profoundly pernicious implications, as many schools treat an IQ in the 70 to 80 range as borderline retarded. By the time such a child comes to Leake & Watts, he or she may have been enveloped by low expectations and unchallenging schooling for as long as 10 years. At this point an irreversible identity has been formed: the child hates school and is utterly without self-confidence. And as school becomes more unrewarding and demeaning, behavior takes a turn for the worse. In the few cases where the school histories are well documented,

one finds comments about a hot temper and fighting going right
back to the first grade.

Another factor working against Paul is that of belonging to
the second generation in foster care. This is an experience that can
hang over a family like a curse in a Greek tragedy. If there is an
established history of begetting children and then giving them up
to foster care, this can become a habitual perception of family
bonds that is extremely difficult to break. In fact I frequently hear
my female students say things such as: "If my kid starts popping shit
with me, I am just going to give it away." The socioeconomic
conditions that create the need for foster care and welfare support
have now been in existence in New York City for several generations. At any given time there are residents at Leake & Watts
whose mother or father has been in foster care. The end of this
problem is nowhere in sight. Over the past eighteen months, I
have watched with dismay as five girls aged 14 to 16 have departed
for a "maternity leave." Infants are then born to mothers with no
husband, with the academic proficiency of a fifth-grader, and aggressive traits of personality that will impede child-rearing or effective career development.

The actual stories of the children of Leake & Watts are variations of the elements contained in these two representative histories. They are all stories of inner city poverty and family chaos.
To the extent that one can document family history, the chaos
appears to go back a couple of generations.

Indeed one of the glaring and incapacitating deficiencies in
the child care field is the lack of documentation and family history.
In this regard the welfare system operates in a timeless present
wherein the past is composed of stupefying catastrophes and the
future bears the dismal fruit of present exertions.

The staggering challenge that faces the foster-care system is to
identify and implement some remedies for dissocial behavior.
There are essentially two avenues along which this work can be
done. First, the agency can try to impose external restraints so that
the children's excesses and aggressions do not have an opportunity
to erupt. These external restraints consist chiefly in creating a
tightly structured environment with precisely established rewards
and punishments. While the external restraints are not especially
curative, they do create a well-regulated environment in which to
make the children aware of their behavior. Then the children can
be encouraged to develop internal restraints so that they bring

their excesses and aggressions under control. This is a therapeutic activity that takes account of the children's weaknesses and seeks to mend them.

Lasting success with these children will come only when they can develop internal restraints to their impulsiveness. For them to do so, however, they have to be enveloped by a predictable and well-regulated environment. One of the principal forces in maintaining this environment is the agency's Behavior Modification (B-Mod) program—an umbrella of reward and punishment that overshadows every phase of a student's life, both in and out of school. As implemented at Leake & Watts, appropriate and responsible acts are rewarded by the accumulation of points, while any failure to meet the program's requirements is penalized by the loss of points. These points are passed out every 40 minutes throughout the school day, and then are fed into a computer along with the points the students have acquired in their cottages and during recreational activities.

A compliant and alert student can acquire 16 points during each 40-minute class period. If, however, the student comes to class and sulks for the period, the reward will be only three or four points. A student who switches back and forth between sulking and studying may find it possible to receive six or eight points. And so it goes, hour after hour, day after day, week after week, until the total runs up into the thousands. The ability to earn high points and stay out of trouble will determine a student's "level," which in turn determines privileges.

It is interesting to note that such behavior modification programs have been in and out of fashion at Leake & Watts for over 100 years. Back in 1916, the year before corporal punishment was finally and categorically forbidden by the Board of Trustees, an elaborate B-Mod system was instituted with levels ranging from A (those with 100 points) to D (those with less than 69 points). One could be fined as much as 30 points for "disgraceful moral behavior," and 10 points for "wearing the wrong clothes" or for "impudence."

The most recent B-Mod program was introduced during the 1987–1988 school year and, although the offenses were not described in the language of biblical condemnation, the form and intention are as they were 70 years ago. Thus we deduct 400 points for minor aggression, 200 points for cursing, and 50 points for cutting class.

In a well-modulated B-Mod class the teacher will be saying, "Nina, you are doing a fine job. You will earn all your points this period." Then the teacher turns with disapprobation toward Ralph and says, "You are paying attention to everyone's business but your own. Keep this up, and you will get zero points for the period." Those who must work with these children on a day-to-day basis find that B-Mod is somewhat like constantly telling someone who stammers, "For heaven's sake, pay attention and stop talking so stupidly," or conversely "That was great. You just did a whole sentence without stumbling." Thus we are constantly drawing attention to a child's weakness, often in a manner that exacerbates it.

There are Skinnerian assumptions at work in B-Mod, in that the control of a person's environment leads to the control of his behavior. We are all creatures of conditioned responses, and—if everything in our environment is an instigation to responsible, purposeful, and disciplined behavior—the desired results will eventually take place. Although the humanist with his belief in autonomy, spontaneity, and individuality will find such Skinnerian schemes repugnant, there is one virtue to B-Mod. It is a system that provides a means to assess a student's behavior. There are students, for example, who habitually cut class, who sleep or refuse work when they do attend, and who drift around the grounds listening to their radios during school hours. When the ineluctable B-Mod computer comes up with its totals, these students come up short in terms that everyone, even the students, can understand. The fact that one student may be earning 150 points a day while another is earning only 12 is inescapable.

Whether or not such a system actually modifies behavior is more questionable. Clearly, some students are more oppositional than others. There are those who are very concerned about accumulating points and, if a teacher appears to waver between, say, a 12 or an 8 for the period, the student will beg, threaten, and cajole, pointing out all the accomplishments of the period. At the other extreme are the students who will refuse work, leave the room without authorization, return 10 minutes later and disrupt those who are working. When the period is over I will make a point of approaching such students with a great show of gusto and beg for permission to autograph their "point card." (The points are recorded on a three-by-five-inch card that each student carries around all day and submits to various teachers, cottage parents, and recreational directors for evaluation.) The delinquent students will be amused by my mock avidity to fill out their card, but then will usually refuse, saying, "Forget it. Points are whack."

Moreover, when it comes to the egregious heights of bad behavior, a B-Mod system is not going to make much difference. The student who will miss no chance to get into a fight is not going to change his ways because he fails to acquire the points that will enable him to buy a candy bar in the school store. Likewise, the student with a hot temper will not pause to calculate point loss before letting loose. A major portion of students' misconduct takes place when they are caught up in the influence of their peers, and at such times they are not concerned with the niceties of the system. Nor is this surprising, as implicit in their conduct disorder is an inability to control impulsive behavior.

The psychiatric literature objects to B-Mod on the basis that conduct-disordered children require internal rather than external restraints. In a sense, all of life is B-Mod. You get a cheaper insurance rate if you do not have any speeding tickets, and you are penalized if you overdraw your bank account. The socialized individual accepts these demands and is able to negotiate them in a competent manner. The dissocial individual, however, will reject these expectations and suffer the consequences again and again. Those who are impelled by a hostile urge to violate the many social contracts that enable civilized life ultimately need to neutralize the aggression itself. There is also the well-documented fact that those who have been maintained under a tight system of external restraints will tend to run wild once the controls are removed. A dangerous or criminal child can learn to negotiate a B-Mod system and earn points, but once he returns to the street, where he does not carry a point card, antisocial behavior can return stronger than ever.

There is always an intrinsic difficulty in implementing a B-Mod system: those who must enforce it do not like it. As a theoretical device to control behavior, it is attractive to administrators and some clinicians. Those who work with the children on a continuous basis, however, often find that wild behavior—when contained within broad limits—is preferable both to endless confrontation over minor infractions and to the depressions that often alternate with wild behavior. I am happiest with my students when they are in high spirits but under control. Those high spirits may well overflow the limits of decorum in the sense that the children are using obscene language or are failing to sit up straight with their feet firmly planted on the floor. I am well aware that if I push them on these matters I may lose what momentum I have. I also vastly prefer their high spirits to those episodes of anger or depression that can cast a pall over everything.

For many of the children there is no middle ground between acting out and extreme depression. A child may arrive for school in the morning in the depths of depression. She will bury her head in her jacket and then sleep at her desk for the first forty minutes of the day. The first sign of improvement is when she looks up with sullen disgust and says, "Howe, I hate that stupid necktie." This is a welcome sign of life and a return to business as usual, and it is not the moment to be overly scrupulous about her affront to my necktie. As a result of many such instances compounded throughout the day, the supposedly seamless fabric of behavior control is rent by small holes of indulgence and connivance.

The real work, of course, is to build up internal restraints, and this is an extremely arduous endeavor. Here is where the most rudimentary building blocks of character development are set in place. The approach of the psychoanalytic experts—Aichhorn, Freidlander, and Anna Freud—is to give the children "compensatory love." If one could but love them as their parents and guardians had failed to love them, one could set them on the way to becoming socialized adults capable of the generous impulses and moral values that make civilization work.

This means that as a matter of policy the agency should endeavor to install concerned and competent adults into the lives of these children on a far-reaching and long-term basis. In the school, for example, all of the students are assigned to a homeroom teacher, and many of them spend as much as half the day or more with the same teacher. Most of their academic needs are met by this one teacher—language arts, math, social studies, sex education, reading. This one adult then becomes answerable for behavior, education, and general progress on as broad a base as possible. The tendencies to exploit the slack within the system, to play adults off against one another, to employ oppositional strategies, to keep an antagonistic distance from adults, to disdain their own worth—all of these are held in abeyance much more effectively by one deeply involved teacher than by a staccato sequence of different teachers.

In the residential life as well, the agency makes an effort to install cottage staff who can play a significant role in the lives of the children. It falls to these workers to see that the children brush their teeth, clean up their rooms, treat one another respectively, bathe, and change their clothes. The real work at a place such as Leake & Watts is done by the people who are with the children every day and try to treat them with the comprehensive solicitude of a parent. This approach is logical and it appeals to our humane feelings. There are indeed many good-hearted people in this work who give of themselves until there appears to be no more to give, and they still go on giving. They do indeed make a difference, but unfortunately they cannot fully reassemble the pieces of a shattered childhood.

For the better part of their lives these children have resisted bonding with adults, as this has been a generally disappointing experience for them. They also know that teachers and social workers are hirelings who receive a salary for being nice to them. Hence they are very quick to recognize and appreciate anything that one does for them beyond the call of duty. When someone cooks something at home and brings it in, they recognize this as something that stands apart. Likewise, a teacher who shows up on days when there is no school will receive a truly heartwarming welcome.

A telling and graphic illustration of the children's true needs arose during a class discussion of birthday party celebrations. For these occasions the homeroom teacher routinely brings in a cake and a token present, for which the school will provide reimbursement. The students were announcing what kind of cake they wanted on their birthdays, when Joy R. suddenly exclaimed, "What I want for my birthday, Mr. Howe, is for you and your family to take me out to dinner and a movie . . . because I know my family won't do it." Joy is a bright, sensitive child with a psychiatrically impaired mother. Unlike many of our children, she is quite capable of forming mature relationships with adults. What she wanted was neither the food nor the presents. She wanted an authentic family experience.

The full extent of this need emerged when I did once hold a child's birthday party at my house. The entire class was present, and we made barbecued chicken. After we finished eating, everyone sat around in embarrassed uncertainty as to whether this was an official school occasion or a family get-together. The question resolved itself when one of the students suddenly asked if I had an album of family photographs. I spent the next half hour with my students examining the snapshots of my own children. They wanted to know about every birthday party and the various members of the extended family who were depicted.

If one can be together with the same group of these children over a period of time and none of them is drastically undersocialized, occasions of this sort can be staged with some regularity. More typically, however, it is not easy to serve up large doses of compensatory love. Even the most patient person will find that there are times when children can be quite unlovable. When they are abusive toward staff members, for example, they will be as sharp and cruel as they are toward their fellow residents. There is no receding hair line, pot belly, overdeveloped breasts, or rickety dental work that escapes their notice. I receive endless jibes about my thinning white hair, my age, my accent, my clothing, and my gait. One must truly let go of all *amour-propre* concerning any aspect of one's life that could be subject to comment or imitation. One of the most engrossing challenges of this work is trying to find the energy and impulse to love children who have such a talent for scourging those who help them.

And then, when they receive kind and loving treatment, they will both test it and exploit it. At the birthday parties at school, I have occasionally added an unexpected treat at my own expense— a beverage or some home-cooked food. If I bring fruit juice, someone will complain that I did not bring soda. If I bring vanilla ice cream, someone will ask for chocolate. They will eat everything in sight and then complain that it was not right. For many of the staff the natural response will be, "Why bother, if they are never satisfied?"

Having undergone so much emotional deprivation and having built up so much anger, the children are simply too hardened and skeptical to open themselves unreservedly to acts of kindness. Before one can restore to them the affection they missed in the formative years of their infancy, one must penetrate a hard shell of anger and resentment. I have come up against just such a shell of resistance with one of my students from a year ago, Trisha M. She had been in my core group for a year and although she had a terrible mouth that seemed to become worse rather than better over the course of the year, we had established a pleasant relationship. This year she is not in any of my classes, and I see her only occasionally in the hallways. Whenever we meet, I try to come up with some pleasantry such as "Hi, beautiful!" or "You're looking great today." For about six months she invariably answered by saying, "Shut the fuck up!" It took that long before she would accept my remarks with reluctant satisfaction. Clearly she was not as interested in my compliment as she was in seeing whether it would survive her abuse. She also wanted to test whether there was any lasting residue from our relationship of the previous year.

One of the small satisfactions of working with these children is that after an indeterminate period of aggression and resistance, some will begin to return kindness with a little more compliance and a little less anger. They will become slightly more manageable, not out of fear of punishment, but out of a desire to please. Thus begins the building up of the internal restraints that had never developed properly in early childhood.

It is sad to note that only under the most favorable circumstances does one reach this first stage of socialization, and then there is rarely the time or the opportunity to advance beyond this first step. By favorable circumstances I mean that not all the staff is equally endowed with goodwill, nor are all of the children equally responsive to it. Some of the staff have simply used up their patience, and some of the children have become so hard of heart that it would require more than an institutional setting to soften their rancor.

The most frequent instances of discernible progress occur when a child arrives at Leake & Watts in a towering rage as the result of some recent rejection or brutality. It is not uncommon, for example for a mother to put her teenage daughter in placement when the daughter has been sexually abused by the mother's live-in boyfriend or new husband. The child will be acutely aware both of the injustice of being assaulted and then the rejection of being thrown out of her home. The mother has sent away her own flesh and blood in preference to a newcomer in the home.

When such a child arrives, she will be unresponsive to adult authority and will greet all discipline and directed activity with curses and resistance. After about a year of shouting epithets at everyone in authority, the child will become more temperate and less abusive. When this happens, it is not simply because the child has been lectured about keeping a civil tongue in her head; it is also because the child has been allowed to cuss out people who maintained a sympathetic interest in her well-being.

Although some old-timers say that when it comes to a

conduct-disordered population they prefer the boys to the girls—the boys are less explosive, and more manageable—I myself find work with the girls more productive. When a girl walks into class surcharged with anger, there is very solid exchange of feelings. This exchange can be trying and exhausting—much more so than the horseplay with the boys—but there is never any doubt that one is dealing with real currency. The payoff from taking on all this passion, however, comes after an extended period of time: it becomes clear that these angry and explosive girls are making progress. The outbursts become less frequent and less intense, and the girls develop the ability to recognize an impending eruption and steer clear of it.

My female students will often tell me with pride of the fights that they did *not* get into. These stories are always very similar. Someone perpetrates a totally unwarranted outrage and the girl feels her temper rising. But then she thinks to herself, "Wait, I don't need this." Despite the fact that the offender deserved to "have her ass waxed," no fight takes place.

As the girls start to progress along these lines, they will start coming to class more regularly, they will take pride in their work, and they will develop the traces of self-esteem. But getting to the first positive signs can take as much as two years, and it is exhausting for the staff who have to come to terms with so much intensity and passion in the course of each school day. In the end, however, it is apparent that the attention and patience of the staff have absorbed and neutralized some of that pent-up passion. All the cursing from the girl and all the gentle remonstrances from the staff have had a healing effect.

The boys, however, only rarely express their feelings with the force and candor of the girls. Over a period of two years they will become more compliant, in the sense of meeting the expectations of the system. They will not get into as many fights, they will be more restrained in cursing out the staff, and they will wreak less willful destruction. In short, they will develop a tacit understanding with the staff that "I won't bother you if you don't bother me." When they do get into trouble, it will be so close to play that no one needs to become seriously involved or invoke major interventions. The end result of this process is a successfully institutionalized child.

The fact remains, however, that even after a couple of years they still do not take their lives seriously, and the underlying pain and anger have been neither resolved nor expended. There has been a personality adjustment that employs levity, machismo, and evasion to negotiate the underlying problems. And to top things off, the staff generally views this as a successful adjustment to the system. We uphold our end of the "I won't bother you" contract by not being overly fastidious about questions of real competence and prospects for survival. Given the compromised nature of life at a residential agency, this ends up being an acceptable arrangement for all parties.

A primary task of anyone who works at a place like Leake & Watts is to absorb some of the pain and anger that were generated at earlier stages of life. The children will arrive in a rage, and those responsible for this anger have in many cases departed entirely from their lives; but the anger is still present and is transferred to those in authority. Thus, cottage parents, teachers, recreation directors, and social workers are subject to anger and abuse they do not deserve. Those staff members who can return curses with kind words, tirades with explanations, and opposition with acceptance are the ones who benefit these children most directly. This is not to say that the residents ever after will use only temperate language; it is only to say that some of the most immediate and uncontrolled antisocial impulses are somewhat blunted by the availability of adults who are prepared to serve as lightning rods for the anger that has been mounting over the years.

"Compensatory love" can also act as a positive force in regenerating moral values. Much of the work with the children is a matter of bringing them back to the stage of life where appropriate development failed to take place. This means that the adults who work with dissocial adolescents must endeavor to engage their affection so fully that the students will come to esteem their cottage parents, teachers, and social workers as they never esteemed their own parents. To the extent that this does happen, the child can be influenced to internalize a better code of conduct.

The problem, again, is time: in a short-term residential treatment center the opportunity to build a deep affective bond, and then to convey a sound moral code, really does not exist. The children generally stay at Leake & Watts for no more than one or two years, and during this time they will be thrown together with a variety of adults in a variety of capacities. Although the children do become very attached to one or another staff member, the system does not have a built-in framework to develop and build on these attachments; rather, such attachments are random occurrences whose therapeutic worth is treated as a serendipity.

In the 1920s, when Aichhorn wrote his *Wayward Youth*, the approach to the problem of dissocial children was colored by the optimism that surrounded the fledgling science of psychoanalysis. Aichhorn believed that by allowing the child to form a strong positive bond with the therapist and other caretakers, the opportunity would automatically arise to rebuild the damage to the ego and superego resulting from defective nurture. The same optimism is to be found in Kate Friedlander's *The Psychoanalytic Approach to Juvenile Delinquency*, published in Great Britain in 1947. By the time one comes to the next major classic in the field, Fritz Redl and David Weinman's *Children Who Hate*, published in 1952, the picture looks somewhat different. The children are of a social class that is radically cut off from middle-class society at large. The problem is no longer one of enabling a temporarily disabled child to reenter a viable environment. The environment that creates the dissocial child is now becoming vitiated by poverty, crime, drugs, unemployment, and broken families. By the time of Claude Brown's *Manchild in the Promised Land* in the 1950s, there is an unmistakably modern picture of crime, poverty, and drug addiction.

Once the dissocial child becomes just another manifestation of a world that has gone wrong, psychoanalysts and psychiatrists begin to withdraw discreetly from the scene. This process has now become commonplace in the treatment of dissocial children. When the psychoanalytic movement first started, it was understood that, in order to be well-suited to treatment, a patient should possess a signfiicant measure of insight and culture. Anyone who works with the children at Leake & Watts is not going to be breaking a sophisticated code of images, poetic phrases, and cultural allusions to unlock the secret workings of the patient's psyche. The children simply lack the detachment to stand apart from their present travail and recognize it as the consequence of their rearing.

As an agency such as Leake & Watts the mode of treatment is perforce a compromise composed of a variety of approaches. On the most immediate level there are the teachers and the cottage staff, who are with the children all the time, and who try to win their compliance with kindness, humor, and gentle persuasion. At the next echelon are the clinical staff of psychiatrists, psychologists, and social workers who endeavor to do some form of therapy with the children and assess whatever remains of their home life. Then at the managerial level there is an elaborate behavior-modification program that seeks to control and monitor the children's conduct with a fixed and predictable repertoire of reward and punishment.

The present situation was foreshadowed by Redl and Weinman back in 1952. Their emphasis is on producing an efficient and functional environment in which to house dissocial children. The concern is not so much with a long-term cure as it is with maintaining the children on a day-to-day basis. Some strategies are destabilizing and others are settling. It is the business of the child-care worker to distinguish between these two and minimize antisocial behavior.

The professionals who deal with these children are not sanguine about sending them back into the world that produced them. In fact, lacking a sound home environment to return to, these children will probably never have a more stable and healthier existence than their term at Leake & Watts. As a result, the mode of treatment is concerned with socializing these children to the requirements of Leake & Watts. Whether this will enable them to negotiate the world that awaits them after they leave is another matter.

For a child to be conduct-disordered is both tragic and crippling. During the day when teaching, I can at times be filled with dismay at how awful these students are. But then, upon reading their case histories after school is out, I am always impressed with the strength and resilience that enables them to be as good as they are.

The children who come to a place such as Leake & Watts have experienced a degree of emotional deprivation that is quite beyond the comprehension of anyone who has had even an approximately normal middle-class upbringing. As a result of the deprivation, the children have developed qualities that make them unlovable to their parents, unmanageable to their teachers, and repugnant to society as a whole.

Although Leake & Watts succeeds in taking some of the hard edge off their aggression, the purely human resources of such an agency are quite inadequate to make good the pain and loss of the early years. The real challenge is in the area of social and economic planning. Depressed socioeconomic conditions are conducive to behavior problems. Where there has been poverty, overcrowding,

foster care, marital discord, a chaotic home life, domestic violence, and a changing cast of primary caretakers, there will be a
tendency toward aggressive behavior and antisocial attitudes. If a
particular group is unable to break out of depressed economic conditions, the dissocial behavior can become a generational curse.
The dissocial child becomes the antisocial adult, who in turn raises
a new generation of dissocial children.

The way out of this generational curse, at least for the earlier
clients of Leake & Watts, had been upward financial mobility. The
big question is whether our society is now either willing or able to
take significant steps against inner-city poverty.

4

Teaching Against
the Grain

To teach the children at Leake & Watts is to discover that education can flourish only in the presence of certain fundamental endowments of mind and spirit. Education is possible for the student who has self-esteem, a belief that the future will be better than the past, and the desire to become a free and autonomous adult. To the extent that any of these qualities is missing, the work of an educator becomes more difficult and less productive.

Any honest account of teaching dissocial children is not going to come across as a touching success story. The few successes I have enjoyed were unexpected and happened under conditions that are generally difficult to duplicate. The real story here is of children whose delight in learning, eagerness for growth, and powers of imagination have been so pinched and thwarted over the years that those who propose to teach them find themselves at the limits of the possible.

The critical fact is that the students' expectations are so low that one cannot influence them significantly by appealing to their will to excel, their desire for personal growth, and their need to function harmoniously with peers and elders. They have not yet developed the healthy adolescent need to define themselves in the adult world and develop demonstrable competence. In this regard they are still in a pre-adolescent stage. As a result, educators tend to provide for them the same classroom environment and teaching techniques that one would employ with children who are, say, 10 years old. This means a highly structured environment, a pervasive system of reward and punishment, and minimal intrusion of the unexpected.

Although there is no way of dealing with these students that is going to be entirely satisfactory, the strength of this approach is that it meets the students at their developmental and educational level and then endeavors to pick up the thread of life and learning where it broke off. The weakness is that in many ways these students truly are young adults and hence know that they are being patronized when they enter a class whose style and content are geared to the needs of a young child. This provokes their resentment and causes them to look down on their schooling. Thus, educators can unintentionally impede the development of the few adult qualities these students do possess.

One of the sustaining forces in my life as a teacher of these children is a perverse fascination with the impossibility of the task at hand. I have always been bemused by the almost demented dedication of Socrates, who was prepared to die in order to instruct people whose capacity for self-improvement he thought to be negligible. I find this approach liberating in that it places the work of a teacher beyond the narrow criteria of success and failure. Teaching becomes a self-sufficient activity that is undertaken for its own sake, not for the sake of the demonstrable good that is being accomplished.

I will generally start my day by trying to get my students to read aloud, either from the newspaper or whatever book we happen to be reading at the time. At present it is a biography of Martin Luther King, Jr., written at about a sixth-grade level. In my class of 10 students there are two I can always count on to read. The others, however, will tell me with varying degrees of conviction that they do not feel well, that the book is stupid, that they wish to be left alone. About half the time the recalcitrant students can be won over to read if I can come up with a sufficient display of concern, indignation, or disbelief. The problem is that one has limited energies for these bouts of persuasion and imprecation and

I am always out of energy well before the school day runs out of periods.

The source for their academic difficulties is to be found in their long histories of bad behavior. For years the students have been so consumed by their needs and difficulties that effective learning has been thwarted by indifference, opposition, and truancy. As a result, on average they are at the 5th- or 6th-grade level, instead of 11th or 12th, where they should ostensibly be. A further consequence is that kids who are quick, responsive, and verbally adroit have failed to develop age-appropriate reading and testing skills, and hence show an IQ level between 75 and 85.

What can an educator do when confronted by such a challenge? An obvious though not very satisfying answer is to create a classroom environment that will hold their oppositional tendencies in abeyance and then offer instruction at their present intellectual level.

There are guidelines implicit in the training of a special educator and there are directives that come down from the administration, and yet each classroom is in all essential matters of style, tone of voice, and toleration for wild antics, a direct reflection of the teacher's personality. Indeed, one of the things I have always appreciated about teaching, at all levels, is the fact that once the door closes behind you in your classroom, you are a sovereign. A teacher alone with his or her students enjoys a degree of autonomy that no other situation can match. In great measure the heart of the teaching experience is an exchange of personal energies, and this is especially true for special education where instruction and nurture overlap. As a result I see a wide range of styles among my colleagues.

There are, for example, some teachers who are quickly offended by bad language, opposition, and the shenanigans of the students. They tend to have a strong interest in controlling their charges and will not even embark on the business of education until a certain modicum of order has been established. At the opposite extreme are those teachers who find the students' high spirits engaging and are willing to conduct classes in the presence of significant chaos. I lean in the latter direction, and yet this may be a mistake to the extent that it places a greater strain on the personal energies of the teacher. In a classroom with rigid rules and expectations, business moves ahead and non-compliant students are removed from the room as necessary. In a looser environment that grants the students more latitude, emotions run closer to the surface and the unexpected erupts more frequently. The teachers who last the longest in this business are the ones who have set clear limits as to what they will tolerate. They will try to distance them-selves from the wildest students and expend their energies only in the presence of acceptable compliance.

On the side of ruling with a firm hand, it can also be said that once order and discipline have been established, it requires less energy to run a tight class than a rowdy one. The stricter teacher has chosen a possible task—short-term behavior management—while the indulgent teacher seeks the more implausible (and only occasionally attainable) goal of tapping the students' suppressed and forgotten resources.

If we are going to take these students back in time for their discipline and treat them as though they were 10 years old, then it follows that the same should be done with their schooling. The hope is that once order has been established, we can then try to achieve at least the rudiments of a functional education. Before moving on to the business of adult life, these students should know how to convert fractions to decimals, they should distinguish be-tween a complete sentence and a fragment, and they should know who Julius Caesar, Abraham Lincoln, and Joseph Stalin were. Offering these students a steady regimen of low-level work presents problems, however.

On the one hand, remedial work is necessary, as anyone who embarks on adult life with only a fourth- or fifth-grade education will be excluded from all but the most menial jobs. With that the curse of poverty and domestic chaos will pass on to the next gen-eration. On the positive side, the school does in fact succeed in getting about a third of its students through the New York State Regents Competency Tests in reading, writing, and math. These tests require a clear nuts-and-bolts proficiency in the three Rs and are an absolute requirement for a high school diploma in the state of New York. And although these tests demand only about a sixth- or seventh-grade level of proficiency, the students who do pass recognize this as a significant milestone in their education.

The problem is that the low-level remedial work, just like the B-Mod program, has a regressive impact. If this is all we do, then we fail to recognize that, whether we like it or not, these students are emerging adults and have many of the same needs as other adolescents. They need to start making appropriate career choices, they need to gain some sense of competence and proficiency, and they need to be acknowledged as young adults waiting to take their place beside the present adult generation.

To batter them over the head day in, day out with long division and the rules about double negatives is to remind them that they are incompetent children. One of my most common problems is with the student who hurls his or her work on the floor and exclaims, "Man, this is baby shit. I'm sick of it!"

When this happens I often feel the impulse to rush over to the desk, trample the papers underfoot, and say, "So much for baby shit." But I can't, as the following incident makes clear.

Last spring I was tutoring one of our most advanced students in trigonometry and my blackboard was full of diagrams and formulas involving sines, tangents, and cosines. While I was doing this two of his friends were out of their regular class, cruising the halls. One of them was a gentle and mild-tempered young man with a serious crack addiction and absolutely no capacity for learning. The other was a rougher and more rowdy type. Both were of an age to be juniors in high school but were four or five years behind.

They looked into my room through the little window at the door and immediately burst in. They took seats and exclaimed, "Hey Howe, this is the move. How come we don't get this in our classes?" At first I tried to get them to leave, as they were truant from their regular classes. When they would not, I explained that I was doing trigonometry. The mellow one said, "This is really interesting. I want to be in your class." Although they had no idea of what I was doing, what the procedures were, or how the answers were computed, they insisted on staying for the entire period, volunteering answers at every juncture.

What they had recognized on my blackboard was age-appropriate work. To see such work presented in their school created the impression, at least for a 30-minute period, that their schooling had not been derailed, that they were not pathetically undereducated, that they might somehow enter the world of adult competence. Once I saw that there was no getting rid of them, I tried to involve them in the session, but lost them in simple matters of multiplication, reducing fractions, and the placement of decimals.

They left saying that it had been a great class and that they would be sure to be present for the next session. Once they left my room, the spell was broken and they did not come back. There are, unfortunately, many revelations of this sort, when it becomes painfully clear that age-appropriate work will cause even eager students to flounder for lack of the basics.

It is generally a manageable task to implement B-Mod and low-level remediation, while it is extremely difficult to come up with an ingenious and revolutionary strategy that can at once both contain behaviors and expedite education. The fact is that there is no easy solution to the problems that arise in connection with conduct-disorders. With conduct-disordered students, some aspects of their cognitive and emotional development advance while others stand still. Many of these students are sufficiently clearheaded to become aware of this disparity and be tormented by it.

As I endeavor to work with my students I often think of the hardheaded perversity of Zen Buddhist philosophy. My job, which is to teach the unteachable, is not very different from listening for the sound of one hand clapping. I have been assigned students who have been floundering in school for most of their lives, and I am told to go in there and teach them. There is in this mandate an implicit contradiction, and the way the Zen aspirant succeeds is to rethink the problem. Teaching has to mean something other than just imparting information, and I must then convince myself that the most pressing educational need of these children is something other than gathering in for them the bits and pieces of a fifth-grade education.

My first concern is to make my classroom into a regenerative and pleasant environment and then see what teaching can be done. Last year I had a homogeneous group of 15- and 16-year-old girls, most of whom were functioning on a fifth-grade level. We would start off each day by taking turns reading aloud from the *Daily News*. Although we learned more about city corruption, "rough sex," and the crack wars than I would have wanted, the paper did in fact represent a coherent response to city life. My emphasis was on creating a civil and harmonious group, and reading a lurid tabloid together did the job. At the start of the year, for instance, the two students who were at second- or third-grade level refused to read aloud. By January, however, they were reading aloud, assisted and prompted by the more accomplished readers.

As the year progressed I tried to neutralize their ennui and opposition with non-academic activities. We had a sewing machine with which we made pillows and stuffed animals. There was a computer with various quasi-educational games, and within a couple of minutes we could set up strobe lights and a background to take photographs of one another.

The following year I tried with great difficulty to employ the same strategies with a very different group. There was a mixture of boys and girls with an age range from 14 to 18, and an IQ range from 57 to 104. By the time the year came to an end, it was clear that the many disparities of age, proficiency, and personality had outsmarted last year's Zen mind. The low-level readers never stopped refusing to read aloud. The sewing machine was viewed with indifference or suspicion, and the brighter, more oppositional students intimidated the slower ones. In this instance obtaining a coherent and cohesive focus was not an attainable goal. I was forced to deal with each student individually, which means that although the group had failed as a class, there were individual pockets of success.

In an attempt to provide as many options as possible, the school mixes various modes of learning. There are some teachers who are answerable for a specific subject matter—say, math or social studies—and they see all the more competent students in the school. Then there are those like myself who have a contained class, which means that I am with the same group of students four or five periods a day and teach them all subjects.

Irrespective of the classroom environment, however, our students have certain learning problems that are particularly pernicious. One of the gravest obstacles they face to acquiring a truly productive education is their unwillingness to tolerate getting stuck or to tackle new material. They will back away from any assignment that they cannot at once understand and accomplish. To get stuck is to observe one's own mind momentarily stretched beyond its capabilities. While this can be stimulating and desirable for a strong and healthy mind, it is not so for students who have met with repeated defeat in their schooling and hence distrust their own capabilities. When they meet with a problem or procedure they do not immediately grasp, they are reluctant to seek help for fear of appearing stupid and then failing to grasp the explanation. If they do ask a question, one of their fellow students is apt to interject something disparaging, such as "Any fool knows that, except maybe your mother, that crusty heifer."

Teachers tend to respond to this situation by giving the students work that lies well within their competence and then presenting it in a manner that is self-explanatory. When I use this format, my procedure is to hand out one sheet of paper with an assignment, another sheet with an exact explanation of how to do the assignment, and a third sheet on which to write out the work. Under these conditions, a perfect class is one in which the students work in silence, interrupted only by occasional announcements that someone has finished the papers at hand.

I will then quickly give the student a new assignment and correct the work on the spot. And the correcting must be done with great restraint and in a manner that implies praise and approval. Thus, what little teaching there is takes place at the moment of pointing out their errors and suggesting ways to avoid them in the future.

In a typical instance, I might pass out a 300-word biography of Louis Armstrong, written for fifth-grade readers. Attached to the biography is a multiple-choice question sheet with boxes for the answer. The student is asked to fill in the box next to the instrument that Louis Armstrong did *not* play: trumpet, cornet, trombone, violin. If all goes well, my better students will do a couple of these sheets in a forty-minute period. They will receive a grade of 85 to 95 with a comment such as "great job" or "keep up the good work" written at the top.

I observe this scenario with mixed feelings. On the one hand I am aware that they are deriving satisfaction from doing work and getting it right. Every now and then, however, one of them will be struck by the same thought that is troubling me and exclaim, "Man, this is stupid. I did this shit back in the fifth grade." At such moments I feel that I have indeed tricked them into doing stupid work and what they don't know about fifth-grade reading comprehension is the least of their problems.

This technique of "quiet seat work" is popular for the same reason as B-Mod: it addresses short-term compliance rather than long-term growth, and it makes lighter demands on staff energies than real, stand-up teaching. One of the torments of dealing with dissocial children is that the human contact they most need is the very thing they resist and subvert. What they really need is a teacher who will face them, seek eye contact, deflect their jibes and evasions, and tell them what they need to know. To the extent that one helps them, it is largely because adults will step into the line of their oppositional fire and address their needs. Such work, however, is so arduous that treatment is generally broken up into manageable and impersonal segments, supported by strategies that insulate frontline workers from intolerable levels of abuse and frustration.

Whenever possible I try to move away from the handouts and offer a more direct presentation. The students will take turns, for example, reading aloud from their biography of Martin Luther King, Jr. Every sentence or two I will stop the proceedings to consolidate. "What was Martin Luther King's highest degree?" "Where did the first bus boycott take place?" "What does the word boycott mean?" "Where did he learn about nonviolence?" At first I will ask these questions of the more alert and attentive students. Then once I see that they know what is going on, I will ask the same questions of the sleepers, the talkers, and the disrupters.

I will sit on their desks, I will shake them by the shoulders, I will hurl chalk against the wall, I will interpose my chair between two gossiping students and butt into their conversation. If they are not depressed on that particular day, they will find my antics amusing and pay attention—not so much to the academic content, as to my performance. If I can find the strength to carry on like this for forty minutes, I can convey most of the material to most of the students. The trouble is that such performances are enormously draining and I am good for only one or two a day.

This approach has the advantage of engaging the students on a personal level and giving them the pleasure of reciting something they have just learned. The problem is that there are another six periods in the day during which my strength suffices only for a more pedestrian and tedious presentation.

They drift through much of their schooling in a semi-compliant, semi-interested, semi-somnolent daze. An incident that brought this home to me occurred during a recent summer session. Since there are not many satisfactory texts in this field, there is always the likelihood of students being asked to repeat work. During the summer program I would supervise my core group while another teacher gave them language arts instruction. On one occasion I noticed that the teacher was giving them handouts I had used with the same group six weeks earlier. It was in fact one of our fourth-grade reading tests—perhaps 300 words about the life of Arthur Ashe followed by multiple choice questions on his country of origin, why he chose to live in California, and what trophies he won. After the usual coaxing and cajoling needed to get the class under way, my students proceeded to do the work. Either they failed to notice or chose not to notice that they had done the same exercises less than two months earlier. As usual they received their grade of 90 or 95.

There was absolutely nothing memorable about the work. It had been routine and easy six weeks earlier. There had been no significant challenge or problem to solve. On both occasions the experience had been no more stimulating or notable than, say, eating a hamburger.

Beyond this, the tight structure and the pervasive presence of restraints to their acting out had the effect of anesthesizing curiosity and the spirit of inquiry. Once again the particular dilemma of this kind of education arises. To educate them at their level is to stultify and antagonize them. The conventional wisdom favors a well-regulated environment in which the children can perform manageable tasks—even if this does extinguish curiosity and deaden the spirit. The education that is mandated keeps the children busy, keeps them in school and, in the best of instances, elevates their competency level by a year or two. Thus over a two-year period an 18-year-old will have advanced from a fourth-grade to a sixth-grade level of competence.

Once behavior is marginally under control and the children are sitting at their desks with pencils poised, yet another problem arises. They are reluctant to advance their intellectual level beyond their emotional level. Sometimes I will come across students, particularly among the girls, who have become readers as a defense against pain and depression. Because of their appetite for books, their reading level shoots up to that of a college freshman. This past year I have had two girls in my class, one aged 14 and the other 16, whose reading comprehension was on a post-high-school level.

I fancied that I had found an opportunity to engage students at a challenging and age-appropriate level. I made my overture by telling them I was going to give them the real schooling they had always demanded: Hawthorne, Steinbeck, Hemingway. Nevertheless, I simply could not get them to look at anything beyond the level of Nancy Drew. I could count on them to hand back any book that did not have a picture on the cover and large type.

The same resistance was true for areas other than literature. I acquired a college text on world history for one of my high-level readers, and at first she was excited to learn new terms such as "Cro-magnon" and "paleolithic." Then, after about two weeks, she began to find the material disquieting, even though it was well within her competence. I tried for some time to coax her ahead and then finally sought out a ninth-grade level book on the same topic with four-color drawings of cavemen and review questions at the end of each section. Although she continued to be as truant and work-resistant as ever, the book was no longer the problem. When she was available for work, she did move ahead with this book. "Implements" were now "tools," "Cro-magnon" and "pithecanthropus" were now "cavemen," and there was nothing of sympathetic magic, the origins of ritual, or the cave paintings of Lascaux.

I had the same student for language arts, and the problem was even more pronounced here. I gave her a reader that was about two years below her reading level—grade 11—that contained short stories followed by questions about character, motivation, plot, and style. This was all new to her and would raise her ability to new limits. She absolutely refused, and then went on to describe the reader she had used in sixth grade. If I could get her a book like that one, she said, she would work.

I managed to secure a set of 4"-by-6" readers with large type and simple line drawings at the beginning of each story. The multiple choice questions at the end of each story were totally non-interpretive in nature. "Mr. Smith was able to help the Jones family because: 1. He was a carpenter. 2. He had a lot of money. 3. He knew how to fly an airplane. 4. His house was nearby." As promised, she did her work, totally unconcerned about the fact that she was functioning about six years below her proven reading level.

This experience has repeated itself with minor variations. It always involves a student whose cognitive abilities are well in advance of the subject matter he or she is willing to take on. In such instances I feel that they are being held back by a retrograde pull from the past. With each passing year life has become more complex, more confusing, more unmanageable, and more intolerable. Their experiences have already branched out into an extended web of ramifications that has taxed their mind to the limit. To move ahead to the next level of intellectual mastery is to run the risk of meeting a whole new array of confusing adversaries. What they are telling me with their demands for easy books is that they want to slip back to a time when things seemed less threatening and more intelligible.

One manifestation of this retrograde tendency is the pervasive presence of thumb-sucking. There are times when I will show a movie in my class on a VCR. Once the lights go down and everyone is absorbed, I will notice that fully a third of the class are sucking their thumbs. Some of these are girls who have sold their bodies and boys who have hustled drugs. Beneath the tough exterior and the grim experiences there is a small child looking for lost innocence.

Another problem is the students' extremely short attention span. Due to their aversion to schooling and their quickness to become distracted and get into trouble, they can commit their attention to their work only for very brief intervals. As a consequence it is difficult for them to develop serious and abiding interests. One does not see them discovering a passion for ham radio, mystery novels, computer hacking, or the arts. Since their education must be broken up into small parcels that can be assimilated in ten to twenty minutes, they lack the opportunity to immerse themselves in a subject and to become absorbed by it. Only occasionally do the students experience proceeding from small and discrete pieces to major chunks of real learning. And in the absence of this experience, they lack an age-appropriate sense of expertise and competence. If they continue to convert fractions to decimals, answer true or false questions about their reading, and do art and crafts projects that can be completed in a matter of one period, what is the likelihood of such an education engaging their interest? Will they ever develop significant abilities and be able to view themselves as competent adults?

Generally speaking, the answer is no. There are occasional exceptions and, as is so often the case, they occur under conditions that are hard to anticipate or duplicate. Much work in fact needs to be done in curriculum development to prepare students who lack traditional academic skills for vocations that rest on nontraditional skills and still are at least modestly prestigious and well paid.

In order for education to become a powerful force in the life of an adolescent, students must command significant powers of imagination and the ability to immerse their narrow and immediate world into a broader realm of thought and inquiry. Unfortunately for our students, the capacity for abstract and speculative thought is underdeveloped.

According to the French developmental psychologist Jean Piaget, persons in their mid- or late teens enter the stage known as "formal operations." To be capable of formal operations is to have the capacity for hypothetical thought and empathy. Thus an intellectually mature student in late adolescence can absorb a work of fiction and assess the importance of the characters to her own life. Such a student can read a lyric poem about falling in love or the shortness of life and then venture into the reality described in the poem, while a student with immature intellectual growth will lack the imaginative powers that enable this experience.

Such immaturity all but precludes the study of literature. Fiction and poetry, both products of the imagination, require readers who can detach themselves from the immediate reality of the personal and the concrete. Having found literature to be the most formative element in my own education, I keep making efforts to make readers out of my students. If I have them take turns reading aloud, if the text is directly pertinent to their own experience, and if I stop periodically to inquire whether anyone has had an experience similar to the one being described, there will be occasional moments of recognition. There are some poems by Langston Hughes, particularly those about the dignity and suffering of the black people, that will at least briefly hold their attention. My most successful literary text to date has been Claude Brown's *Manchild in the Promised Land*. This is a biography that tells the students' own story—the street scene, drugs, petty crime, poverty, and a devastating home life, all culminating in foster care. This book does strike their fancy and they frequently ask me to read aloud from it. If the right mix of students is present, they will remain quiet for as much as 20 minutes while I read aloud about the protagonist "jugging the funky chicks" around 146th Street and Seventh Avenue.

Occasionally my students will become so absorbed that they will ask me to lend them the book. I have procured additional copies, but of the half dozen who have borrowed the book, only one actually did any reading in it. The sustained interest was not there, nor was there anything in their mode of existence that would allow the time and energy for serious reading.

Moreover, my attempts to draw them into discussion are basically unavailing. I try to get them to compare the street life of the 1950s with their own experiences. Was it more violent, less violent, more guns, fewer guns, more drugs, fewer drugs? If things are going well in class and no one has become disruptive, they may start comparing notes about where to hide out overnight if things are too hot at home. They will also reminisce about getting kicked out of school, starting fights, cussing out teachers, and playing truant. Since they have little patience with listening to one another, these discussions have to be brief—they are much more entertaining for me than for the rest of the class. Thus, although their reading can be suggestive for them, they have a hard time understanding their own lives in terms of someone else's life as depicted in a book.

These students are so unaccustomed to literary expression that from time to time they will actually ask me to show them the book. I will be reading a particularly salty passage about pounding someone in a back alley or running a train on a hooker who has been holding money back from her pimp, and someone will exclaim, "Come on! Does it really say that? Let me see the book." I will then circulate the book around the room, pointing to the passage in question. They simply want reassurance that something as remote and abstract as a book can speak so directly to life as they know it. These are students for whom the distance between the printed page and the experience of life itself is very nearly unfathomable.

Unfortunately, my success with Claude Brown was unique. Even Richard Wright's accounts of growing up in the south were too remote and hence too abstract to be of interest. To read them the myths of ancient Greece, which I never did, or the folk tales of nineteenth-century black America, which I did, is to place them in such an alien frame of reference that their attention wanders almost at once.

I still try from time to time to introduce works of literature in hope that a new author, a new approach, or new subject matter will overcome some of their resistance. To date, however, fiction and poetry continue to meet with opposition unless they happen to portray feelings and experiences immediately familiar to my students.

When I first started teaching at Leake & Watts and was not yet aware of how limited my students' speculative powers are, I became enthralled with the prospect of offering a course on morality. My thought was to posit questions of right and wrong to them and then we would work our way together toward a solution. What an opportunity, I thought, to probe and expedite the process by which one becomes a moral person. I would discuss with them the various forces that govern our conduct—self-interest, affection toward friends and family, altruism, and perhaps even a religious code. I would then propose moral dilemmas in hope of finding a basis for their resolution. The course was a total washout. When presented with a moral problem, they would always elect the path of self-serving expedience. I was aware that their personal conduct was in many cases nowhere near as bad as the code they were espousing. Most of them are in fact capable of sharing or giving up something they want and anticipating the needs of others.

A touching display of this altruism has emerged in the matter of passing out candies. Every now and then a student will nudge me in the halls and without saying a word will press a candy into my hand. They will not allow my morning candy-dispensing routine to go unnoticed and unrequited. If I do not eat the candy right away, but put it in my pocket, I will be told, "Make sure you eat that and don't go giving it to someone else." And if I run into the same student later on during the day, I will be asked, "How was the lollipop I gave you, Howe?"

There is also a certain reckless generosity with cigarettes. One student will ask another for a cigarette and receive the answer, "Come on, man, this is my last one." The latter will then take it out of a pocket or from behind an ear, gaze at it dolefully, and say, "O shit, go ahead and take it." This may seem like a small matter, but such pleasures are few and significant. For many the highlight of a day in school may be the cigarette break.

In my ethics course, however, I was not able to convince them that they were not in fact as bad as they claimed they were. The failure of the course derived from their abject self-image—it would strike them as fake and out of character to take a moral stance. Also—and this is the tragic aspect for an educator—I could not get them to view a situation in a speculative manner. Although many of them would be willing to lend their coat to a friend on a cold day and freeze as a consequence, I could not get them to recognize in the abstract that altruism had been a force in their lives.

When it comes to abstracting from life to thought, they find it difficult to make the step from general principle to concrete application. For example, many of them are well versed in the Bible and can recite the Ten Commandments from memory. If, however, I depict a moral dilemma such as they might encounter in their daily lives, they are at a loss to reason either deductively from the commandments to the situation or inductively from a situation to the appropriate commandment.

My students have simply not come to the deliberative discernment that befits their age. This is not to say that they will not at some time come into the favorable and harmonious circumstances that will enable this growth to take place. But the point I failed to grasp until after I had given my course on right and wrong was that, for students with undeveloped cognitive and reflective powers, moral action is tangible and immediate, not theoretical and intellectual. What they learn about morality and generosity takes place in the realm of candy and cigarettes, not tracts and discussions.

The first requirement for a teacher who chooses to work with these children is to obtain some degree of compliance from them. Here again there are no easy answers. Such measures as have been employed by educators are tentative, hit-or-miss, or even exacerbate the very problems they propose to solve. The one principle I can affirm without reservation is to give them unqualified affection. These students have two great needs: love and structure. And I find that things go better if love precedes structure in the order of business. By love I do not mean anything unctuous, sentimental, or patronizing. I mean a willingness to accept them unconditionally and show them the approval they have failed to receive from family and society. This is never easy, as most of these children have an irrepressible need to bring their teachers to the moment when they want to throw up their hands and exclaim, "I give up." One of the first steps toward working effectively with these students is to persuade them that such a point will never come. I find that once they are convinced that an adult in authority can maintain an undaunted desire to work for their good, their first level of resistance breaks down.

If these students can be convinced that there is tier upon tier of safety nets to catch them when their behavior runs out of control, a profound and primal step has been taken toward stabilizing their conduct. Unfortunately, many of the students are incapable of such trust, and then the teachers are too quickly depleted of their optimism and kind feelings. Those who do accept the benign influence of adults will then go on to accept, at least to a limited degree, structure and directed activity. The process moves ahead, however, in microscopic increments.

There is no formula or easy answer. Those who enter the

classroom as teachers in this area of special education know that education is a small part of what they do. Indeed I would say that one of the prerequisites for working in this field is the ability to suspend—even expunge—the desire for discernible progress. What counts is being there, and what results from being there is largely obscured by the swarm of daily failures and setbacks. As these students see their teachers appear in class day after day with fresh confidence in the future, one occasionally fancies that there is a slow erosion of their anger, intransigence, and negative self-image.

5

Teaching the Whole Person

Education does best in an atmosphere of anticipation. To embark upon learning something is in essence an act of hope. Even if the knowledge acquired is disagreeable or disappointing, there is the belief that one's life will in some way be clarified or enhanced by it. Without this the usefulness of the entire endeavor can hang in doubt. And then when a teacher does attempt to raise the hopes and expectations of undersocialized students, he is hampered by their inability to form a positive bond with adults. Their relations with adults have been so full of abuse and disappointment that the children have finally taken it personally—they do not believe that an adult can show them serious respect. Thus the two essential features of educating the whole person are to let the students know that there are viable prospects open to them, and to show them that they can indeed enter into a productive and trusting relationship with an adult.

It is only after they have been able to have sustained positive relationships with the adults in their lives that the first glimmer of self-regard begins to appear. One of the books in this field poses the doleful question, "What to do until the ego comes?" Here "ego" means the personality structure of values, priorities, and incentives that determine how we respond to our experiences. A person with a well-developed ego has a clear sense of identity and is able to make firm and coherent decisions about life. A person with an undeveloped ego, on the other hand, will undervalue his aspirations, his achievements, and his relationships.

Effective education requires a well-developed ego accompanied by the conviction that one can accomplish worthwhile goals in life. For such a well-nurtured child schoolwork is not an extraneous and alien activity, but rather a clear and significant means to becoming the person he hopes to be.

One of the great difficulties of teaching the students is that their expectations border on nihilism. Their parents are worse off than their grandparents, and they themselves are generally worse off than their parents were. For them there is something insubstantial in all our preachments about education, self-betterment, a career, and a productive place in society. They tend either to have no conception of the future or to entertain surreal fantasies of high living.

My students have a very telling diversion that I find painful to witness. When they pose to be photographed, they will often hold a piece of paper next to their face with an ID number on it, as in a police mug shot. They never tire of taunting one another about how their picture will end up on the wall in the post office. The real subject of this joke is self-esteem, and I feel that part of my job as their teacher is to deflate whatever humor they see in this joke.

Once I can break out of the unwholesome diversion of having my students pose for police mug shots, there is another highly edifying side to photographing them. They are overwhelmed by the sight of a good photograph of themselves and will never tire of posing for my camera. I often end the week by setting up portrait lighting and a backdrop in my classroom at 2:45 P.M. on Friday—15 minutes before the building closes for the weekend. There are generally 10 to 15 students clamoring to have their photograph taken. When I come in early the following week with album-size prints, the children mob me, but the excitement goes beyond all bounds when they receive enlargements. They use their credit at the school store to purchase 16-by-24-inch poster prints of their portraits, and these are to be seen in their rooms as well as in the homes of their parents and extended family. They pose with a bravado and zest that often leads to excellent photographs. When they see themselves looking confident and stylish, they are quite literally filled with wonder.

I will often find out more than I would like to know when I ask these children what they would like to do with their lives. Almost all of them have a socially acceptable answer—nurse, carpenter, cop—which they will proffer in official situations to social workers, psychologists, and psychiatrists. In their less guarded moments, however, they will show alarming candor. On more occasions than I care to think of, my female students have told me of their intention to become hookers. As they say this, I realize that they want me to be shocked and try to talk them out of it. And yet it is clearly something they have thought about. When I ask my male students about their future, they will often say, "Don't worry about me. I know how to take care of myself." What they are saying is that they know how to make it on the street and they expect adult life to be more of the same.

These visions of crime and prostitution are often vivid in my mind when I am teaching about the digestive tract or the Civil Rights movement. If these students are only half-serious about what they are saying, my edifying discourse on gastric juices or the Fourteenth Amendment falls wide of addressing their most pressing needs.

Here is a richly detailed fantasy by Omar P., a small bright-eyed fifteen-year-old from Brooklyn. Both his immediate and extended family had a long history of trouble with the law, and he would come back from weekend home passes with wild accounts of criminal antics. He lasted with us for about a year before leaving for the streets and, not long thereafter, for prison. This was written in response to an essay assignment to consider what one would do with $100 a day over an extended period of time.

> If I was given $100 a day, I would save it for a month. Then I would have $3,100. Then I would go on a clothes shopping spree. I would buy the freshest clothes that are out. I would buy Balleys (the '87 ones), Benetton, the freshest shirts. Then I would buy some jewelry. I would get some cable with a Mercedes medallion, all gold. [This is a neck chain with the Mercedes star as a pendant, all in massive gold.] Then I would save up my money for three months and buy me a sun-roof 1988 Mercedes with an Alpine radio system with 12 inch woofers for the back. The rest I would invest in some stock. Then I would save up money so when I meet a young girl that

is light-colored, healthy like Dolly Parton, I would not tell her
I have a lot of money because girls like no-juice niggers. I
would buy me a big house like Magic Johnson with a big
screen TV and VCRs in every room. I would get me some
more equipment for my living room and my room. Then I will
put the rest in the bank.

Omar was an extremely competent student and, by the standards of what I normally encounter, this is a reflective and well-
thought-out statement. There is a coherent if unattainable vision
of clothing, automobile, love life, and domestic appointments.

The next piece was written by a sixteen-year-old Hispanic
student, Eddie C. He had been truant, drug-involved, and living
on the Staten Island Ferry before coming to the agency. Once he
had been with us for a couple of years, he began to think about
what he might do with his life. He too was one of our brighter kids
and unusual in the sense that he was able to contemplate questions
of identity and career choices. This was written as an exercise to
prepare for the New York State Regents Competency Test in writing. This exam requires the students to write a coherent and gram-
matical report based upon fragmentary sentences that are presented
out of order. First the student will place a number next to each of
the fragments to determine its place in the finished account and
then will write out the report in order, expanding it with as much
additional narrative as possible. Here are the fragments:

> court date set for August 10
>
> mother afraid he would do something foolish
>
> Freddie was determined to get the camping knife from the case
>
> felt a pair of hands on his shoulders
>
> "I've paid for it. I dropped the receipt," he said nervously
>
> entered the store during lunch hour, as it was most crowded at
> this time of day
>
> arraigned at the station house for shoplifting

Here is the version I received from my student:

> The mother had always been afraid he would do something
> foolish. Freddie was determined to get the camping knife in
> the display case. He entered the store during lunch hour, as it

was most crowded at this time of day. He felt a pair of hands suddenly take hold of his shoulders. "I've already paid for it. I dropped the receipt," he said nervously. He was taken down to the station house and arraigned for shoplifting. The court date was set for August 10. Freddie was put in jail for one year. He got out of jail and got a job in a fish store. Freddie got married and his little boy did the same thing.

By the way, Eddie passed the writing RCT within six months of writing this piece and has had no trouble with the law. The dark humor at the end, however, is more than just a flippant wisecrack. A teacher is a product of the middle class and has faith in upward mobility. When we talk about jobs, careers, and a responsible existence, we are failing to ask ourselves how a child who has seen only poverty, welfare, and chaos is going to view the future. Most success stories start in the home when parents regale their children with visions of their adult life. There is an implied promise of growth and ability when a parent says to a child, "You can be a brain surgeon or an astronaut or anything else you want."

I have yet to find a student in this population who has a realistic notion of what he might become. Theirs is a spectrum that has two ends and no middle: either crime, poverty, and the streets, or some extraordinary bonanza that opens the door to high living.

These two pieces present opposing aspects of the expectations and aspirations these students harbor. All of this turns out to be essential information for the educator, whose job it is to build a bridge from past to present to future. Under ideal conditions education will take place within a sequence of attainable goals leading to a viable future. In this sense education at the high school level is a highly pragmatic activity that teaches adolescents how to negotiate the adult world. Unfortunately these children know only the desperate street life of which the consummation is the gold chain, the Mercedes medallion, and the brand-name sneakers.

One of the goals of effective education is to give these students a realistic sense of what they might become as adults. This year for the first time we have such a program for them, and it has met with resistance and anger. Counselors from the program come to my class once a week and show videos of street-tough inner-city kids going to interviews, dealing with employers, and breaking away from their street cronies. The protagonists in these films learn to stop popping their gum on the job, recall their math skills from school, start getting up early enough in the morning to get to work on time, and tell their old buddies from the neighborhood to wise up and get a job. It is all very plausibly done, and yet my students hate it, as the children in the films show a degree of confidence and self-control that lies beyond their own present capability. They think that if this is what it takes to get a job, "you can count me out."

The counselors now come to my classroom with great trepidation, as I have never seen my students more discourteous and hostile. The counselor will start off the period by stating, "Today we will see how you should behave and dress for an interview." My students will respond by saying, "Get the f———— out of here with your whack-ass videos." They have become a little more compliant over the last couple of weeks, now that they see that the job team is not going to be driven away. I find, however, that on those occasions when my students have received career coaching, they are work-resistant and angry for the rest of the morning. What we are failing to recognize is the enormous distance between my students' present expectations and the expectations of the person who is able to subordinate his or her language, attire, and attitude to the necessity of obtaining employment. This is not to say that career-counseling cannot be done. It does mean, however, that the first goal for these children must be a radical reevaluation of their lives and their self-worth.

A further obstacle to involving the students in their own education is their natural tendency to reject their instructors as irrelevant and extraneous to their most pressing concerns. To believe in and accept the influence of an adult, a child must be convinced that the adult can be counted on to act in his best interest. This turns out to be an enormous and daunting piece of work.

When I first came to Leake & Watts I soon learned how far I would have to reach in order to touch these students. I used to pass out a questionnaire to new students in which I asked them, among other things, what they would like more than anything else. One of the most frequent answers was, "to be left alone." By this they meant, "Spare me your meddlesome attention." As soon as they were old enough to get into trouble—typically, by the first grade—teachers, social workers, and psychologists had been asking them to account for themselves, so any new attempt to get them to do so brought back painful recollections of chaotic family life.

When, therefore, I try to engage my class, this often flies in the face of their wish to be left alone. When education is taking place under optimum conditions, a gratifying experience for everyone concerned is that a student will open up her life at all levels to the influence of a teacher. These students, however, have been unwanted, they have low self-esteem, and they have found many of the key adults in their lives to be contemptuous and abusive of them. As a result, adult relationships can be superficial or dismissive. One of my most important tasks is to help my students accept and profit from the influence of the adults in their lives. A most potent force in education is a spirit of emulation and affection that proceeds from the younger generation to the older. In its absence, much of the purely personal impetus of learning is removed.

A gratifying experience that has now occurred a couple of times is for my students to give me a memento to thank me for my concern. Two years ago I had a class consisting of eight girls ranging in age from 16 to 18. Most of them were rather impulsive and angry, but I could at least speak with them. At the end of the year they gave me a plaque they had made in the school woodshop, in which they thanked me for "being there."

This year I have an extremely resistant and hard-headed group of boys, aged 13 to 15. There is no group I find more intractable than young male adolescents, and yet five months into the school year they threw a party for me out of their own funds. They arranged to have one of the hall monitors take me out of my room for 15 minutes, and when I came back there was ice cream, chips, and soda spread out on my desk. On the wall a computer-generated banner read "Thanks for teaching us, Howe."

Both these incidents would have been less likely to occur in a class with children who had experienced healthy nurture. The children at Leake & Watts have had so little experience with adults who will persist and stay put that when it does happen, it is cause for celebration. It would require an incalculable accumulation of such experiences for these children to reassemble all the lost pieces of trust and self-esteem—which is not to say it could not be done.

Both episodes get to the heart of what I consider to be the effective teaching process with dissocial children. The task is not so much a matter of conveying new knowledge and information as it is of convincing them that an adult could assume a serious commitment to their welfare and development.

When I first started working at Leake & Watts, I was teaching several classes, and I tried to interject a civil degree of concern, involvement, and empathy in my dealings with the students. I would ask them how they felt. I would compliment them on their appearance. I would ask them how their weekend had been. I was so unequivocally and bluntly rebuffed, however, that I ceased to do this. The general response had been, "Mind your effing business." It was not long before I began to pull back.

This in turn led to the period during which I would pass out the self-explanatory handouts and write "Good Work" at the top when they were completed. As time went by, however, I found this to be sterile and ultimately intolerable—which must be how the students view it all the time.

It was only after I was given a self-contained class—five periods with the same group—that I began to realize that "Mind your effing business" might in fact be an invitation to inquire more deeply into their lives. It also became apparent that even the most angry and embittered child does not get much satisfaction from telling people to get out of his life. These students are always engaged in a winnowing process, seeking to know who of the staff can be kept at a distance with a foul-mouthed rejoinder and who will disregard this and take the next step. Hence, an important part of educating the whole person is to let it be known that you wish to be counted among those adults who will come back for more.

The staff's response to abuse represents a continuum rather than two opposing camps. At one extreme are those who keep their distance, engage with the students only in matters of academic interest, and remain at the periphery of their lives. At the other extreme are those whose own lives and limits are ill-defined, and these involve themselves with the students fully and indiscriminately.

The position one takes within this continuum is determined by purely subjective matters of style and personality. I find that the students do not particularly care for the more rigid and distant staff members as they merely serve as impersonal sign posts and enforcers within the system. The more lenient and accessible staff members are better liked and are generally appreciated as being "cool." These students are shrewd enough, however, to have an instinctive aversion to those at the indiscriminate end of the leniency scale. The staff who fail to create effective boundaries can introduce more chaos than these students can tolerate. In my experience, what works best is a posture that sets standards but is willing to start over again and again if the standards are violated.

There is nothing like being thrown together with the same group of students for several hours a day to prove the need for intense engagement, no matter what the personal cost. During my first year with a contained class I found that I was forced to close much of the distance between myself and my students. My cool pleasantries about their weekend or their appearance were taken seriously and their abusive replies about minding my effing business were indeed "an expression of hope." Over the course of the year I discovered that teachers willing to pick their way through a minefield of abuse and anger will find among their students a profound need to bond and connect.

This bond, however, leads only very indirectly to educational gains. One incident with my core group last year could serve as a textbook case study for the role of motivation, bonding, and self-esteem of dissocial students. Shortly after the middle of the year, there were mutinous stirrings in my class. Teachers make a practice of taking their core group off the school grounds on trips to museums, theatrical performances, and points of cultural interest. Here it was February and I had never taken my group on an outing. As I started up the class for the day, one particularly outspoken and aggressive girl who, like many of the most oppositional kids, could also be very charming and beguiling, announced menacingly, "Don't even think of it, Howe. We're not working today." I asked why not and she said it was because I had not yet taken the class on a trip. She went on to say, "We like you, Howe, and that is why we do your work. But if you won't take us on a trip, we're not going to do anything."

I knew she was right about the trip, but I found her choice of words so interesting that I did not want to let the matter rest with a simple capitulation. So I asked, "What do you mean 'my work?' This is your work, and you're not doing it for me. You're doing it for yourselves."

She was totally unresponsive and accused me of quibbling to avoid taking them on the trip. I immediately promised the trip and told them where we would go and what we would eat. Even after the trip was no longer an issue, however, there was nothing I could say that would convince them that they were doing the work for themselves. The fact that they were doing the work "for me" bears out one of the most compelling theories on managing dissocial children—that the only effective way to get them to better their lives is to win their affaction. Although they lack the self-esteem to work on their own behalf, they can be induced to do it out of their esteem for another person. Here lies a truth of great consequence for special educators. Even more than instruction and discipline, our job as educators is to gain the affection of our students. This then becomes the sustaining force that will make up for their lack of motivation and self-regard.

I am engaged right now in a tug-of-war with one of my students, and the resolution is nowhere near in sight. Lenny M. is very bright, irresistibly driven to inflict pain on his peers, and exceptionally accessible to bonding with adults. I have taken his intelligence seriously and am constantly thrusting age-appropriate tasks on him. He in turn speaks of his desire to be challenged in a manner commensurate with his intelligence. I have been teaching Lenny to generate curriculum materials on the computer and have even secured a work-study salary for him.

He is greatly flattered by the confidence and attention, but simply cannot maintain his energy and conviction over a long period of time. About a month ago he failed to show up at the appointed time for his computer work. At the end of the period he came into my classroom and handed me an elaborately lettered note that he had been working on for the last hour in the art room. It read:

> *Dear Quincy,*
>
> *I thank you for what you have done and have tried to do for me. I am trying to let you know that I give up. Sorry!!*
>
> *Love,*
>
> *Lenny*

Since presenting me with this letter, he resumed work on the computer, only to resign once again a couple of weeks later. At issue are his doubts, both as to whether he can do the job and whether I will continue to believe in his abilities. My job as his teacher is very clear to me at this point. I must endlessly reiterate my confidence that he can do it and overlook his defections and lapses. Here the agenda is neither instruction nor getting a specific task accomplished. The goal is to create a sufficient bond of trust and expectation that Lenny will be able to sustain his motivation. If such experiences can occur with sufficient frequency in the life of a child such as Lenny, then one can begin to think about real learning as an end in itself.

Unless a child has a firmly established a degree of self-esteem, we err in talking about advancing toward clearly defined goals. Only very rarely do I hear a student say with conviction that he is going to school with a view toward attaining some specific personal goal. The students will work because they have to, because they are bored, or because they have been begged or cajoled. And those who adapt successfully to institutional living will creep ahead through low-level work while applying the minimal acceptable exertion.

Yet another obstacle facing teachers in this field is the absence of the conventional connection between education and cultural identity. The goal of a humanistic education is to arouse in students the desire to emulate certain instances of humanity functioning at its highest potential. This happens best in cultures where there is a shared consensus about norms of behavior and canons of excellence. Thus a Greek or Roman would look to the conduct of Hector or Aeneas and find a worthy model. Although our present literature is no longer classic and traditional in this sense, a white American can find meaning and guidance in the works of, say, Melville, Twain, or T.S. Eliot.

For the black American, however, the concept of a cultural heritage is still being developed. Although the Black Muslims, African-American scholars, and books like *Roots* make an attempt to connect to a proud and distant past, the education of American blacks is still hampered by a shortage of curricular materials that would define the black cultural heritage and make it acessible to students.

Although there is no lack of gifted and persuasive black writers, there is lack of a unified perspective that will be intelligible to dissocial students. Thus, W. E. Dubois and James Baldwin are simply too literate for them. Richard Wright deals with a period in the black experience that is already history. There are, to be sure, moments of resonance with Langston Hughes, but even these are too disconnected to form a coherent whole for my students. I have tried to present to them the life of Malcolm X and there are aspects of it they find engaging, especially the regeneration from convict to international spokesman. On the other hand, the Islamic frame of reference and the radical criticism of white society are disturbing for them.

My students may take an interest in public figures such as Mike Tyson and Eddie Murphy. They also have a certain anxious and ambivalent regard for the crack lords of the city. The one personage, however, who has been unequivocally enshrined in their imagination is Martin Luther King, Jr. When discussion turns to the Montgomery bus boycott or the march on Washington, these students are neither flippant nor dismissive. These are facts of history no less than the attack on Pearl Harbor or the New Deal, but they possess a gravity that exempts them from the usual complaints that everything is stupid or boring or both.

From time to time I am made aware of what a devastating experience it is to have grown up black in New York City. Usually I get to see this by way of comparison between students who have and have not been reared in New York. There is an aspiration among American blacks about rising above their abject conditions and claiming the prize of achievement and autonomy, more typical of the South than of the Northern cities. Here is a piece written by one of my students who spent much of her life in the South.

> Hi, my name is Passion. I loves to be friendly with people but some people like to take me for a joke, but I don't like that very much, so I am not going to say anything to anybody for ever and ever again.
>
> The Leake & Watts school system stinks and I don't like it a bit. I want to be smart so I can get a good paying job because I want to show my mother that I could do good on my own without her help and when I get that big chance I'm going to jump right at it and show the world I can do it and all black people are not dumb and stupid. We can still show the white man and woman we reached the promised land and we are not climbing back down again for no one. We made it and we are going to carve our names on the big land.

The experience of living in the northern cities has deprived blacks of much of their visionary sense of expectation and deliverance. Incidentally, my students with roots in the South have generally been more teachable and have had a greater ability to perceive their lives as being at least somewhat within their control. By contrast, I find that those students whose families have been in the city for two or more generations are beset by a nihilism that makes the work of education exceedingly difficult.

"Passion," as she calls herself, arrived at Leake & Watts with a terrible temper and a penchant for getting into fights. From the time I met her, however, she had taken it into her mind that she was going to bring her temper under control, behave in class, and get placed in an outside school. Within a year and a half she had accomplished all of these goals. The last time I saw her I was standing in the hallway of our school building and heard someone shout "Howie" behind me. I turned around just in time for her to hurl her considerable weight on me in a flying hug. She had left about four months earlier and could not wait to tell me how well she was doing. "Passion" is someone who had not lost that sense of noble suffering and high hope that has been the legacy of the black South and the Church. It is not clear what is going to replace this experience for the black families who have come to the northern inner cities.

Education can be defined as the attempt to validate one's identity. An issue that extends far beyond special education and the children of Leake & Watts is the need to make available a powerful and elevating curriculum for black Americans. In the absence of this, the formative aspect of their schooling takes place in something of a cultural void, and this is especially unfortunate when working with children whose personal histories have been grievously weighted down by pain and degradation.

One of the things I value about working at a school like Leake & Watts is the fact that my job as a teacher encompasses the lives of my students in the broadest possible way. Learning in this context is more than just acquiring new information; it is creating the entire foundation upon which motivation, hope, and self-regard stand.

6

Teaching for Results

Despite the endless tide of failed endeavors and obstacles to learning, I find that I am able to stand back periodically and recognize that some things work better than others. I find, for example, that providing active instruction is more productive than passing out dittos and workbooks to be done as "quiet seat work." I also find that if I can shift the center of gravity toward work that is concrete, accessible, and immediately gratifying, the students learn more and like it better.

When I am able to break out of the academic regimen and offer instruction in other areas, there is an immediate surge of interest on the part of the students. My first experience of this was in the summer program a couple of years ago. The summer program is somewhat more loosely structured than that of the school year, with the result that there is some degree of freedom in moving students in and out of classes. One of the subjects I teach is photography, and for a couple of weeks I had a sort of a pirate operation where I would take three kids from their regular classes and have them do darkroom work with me. They were becoming increasingly accomplished, and every day they would pester me to get a pass from their regular teacher so they could work with me.

I finally decided that we should make this official, obtain the sanction of the principal, and offer some words of encouragement to the students concerned. I told the principal, who was thrilled to have a teacher come to him with good news about a student rather than bad. He summoned the three students and myself to his office and announced that only on the rarest occasions does a teacher show up in his office with students asking that they be praised rather than censured. He went on to commend the students on their proficiency, their attention to detail, and their willingness to be instructed in a difficult and demanding craft. He of course approved the schedule change and then went around the room to shake hands with each of us.

When the appointed time for our session came around that afternoon, all three of them cut class. Clearly much of the appeal had resided in the fact that this had been a pirate operation without expectations or the pressure of compliance. Now that photography instruction was bolstered by the threat of being marked absent, my students had to let me know that just because they were eager to do photography, they were not going to give up their wilful ways. To their credit, however, I was able to buttonhole all three of them the next morning and get them to show up regularly thereafter. Somehow the pirate flavor of our initial meetings lingered on, and they in fact made good progress in mastering darkroom techniques.

When the fall semester started up again, however, I lost two of the three. Once they were caught up in the regular academic program, they lacked the interest to lobby for continued work in photography. Only one of them, Alberto O., continued to pester me about photography as he had done during the summer session.

My history with Alberto went back to the previous spring semester when I had offered a course in photography to about ten students. The experience was catastrophic and I never did it again for a full-size class. When we were taking pictures, they all wanted to handle the camera. When we were in the darkroom, they all wanted to run the enlarger. Those who were not on the enlarger wanted to see how the chemicals tasted. When I stood up before the class to explain emulsions, lenses, and photochemistry, they would shout me down with, "This is boring. We want to take pictures." It was the typical special ed situation: everything was reduced to classroom management.

As an academic subject photography was too unstructured, with too many shifts between application and theory. When the semester came to an end, I heaved a sigh of relief and vowed never again to set myself up for such a debacle. It was not until the dust settled and summer school began that I discovered that Alberto had been thoroughly fascinated by the photographic process and wanted more. I then made sure that he was a part of my three-man pirate operation in photography.

Alberto has since assumed a unique position among the students I have taught. He is blissfully heedless of all academic instruction and simply refuses to advance himself beyond his fifth-grade capabilities. He has a compliant nature, and rather than cause teachers indignation, he is happy to sit for hours, day after day, going through third-and-fourth-grade workbooks. In photography, on the other hand, he has found a plausible and desirable goal for his adult life. This fact has now become a real stimulus to his education even to the extent that I can now give him text books on photography. He has applied himself continuously over a two-and-a-half year period and, although he was not exactly industrious, he did become a competent darkroom worker capable of turning out acceptable prints.

When I try to teach him theory, he has a hard time grasping things like focal length, aperture ratios, and film sensitivity. He will take notes, he asks questions, and he regularly announces—half to himself and half to me—that this is what he is going to have to learn for his life as a photographer. Unfortunately I am unable to convince him that better math and reading skills will reinforce his grasp of photography. He is satisfied with his present level of competence, which is now far greater in photography than in anything else he has done. Moreover, he sees no need to contaminate this experience with tiresome exercises from math and reading. The fact that he did not pursue his conventional schooling more avidly takes nothing away from his success with photography. Alberto was exceptional among my students in that he had discovered an inherent interest in a subject and was able to view this interest as a possible career goal—something others at the school are generally unable to do.

When he reached the age of 18, his time at the agency had run out and he left us. Since he had never gone beyond his fourth-grade readers, he had no high school diploma. He has come back a couple of times since his discharge in hope of getting help to find employment in a commercial photo lab. If this does happen—and I am working on making it happen—Alberto will be the first student who, despite consistently unacceptable behavior and lack of a high school diploma, succeeded in obtaining a semi-skilled job.

There has been other photography students, but none more persistent than Alberto. The results, with one exception, were the same. They simply failed to take an interest in the subject and felt that they were doing me a favor if they managed to keep busy. Missing in these students was that part of education of "the whole person" that addresses motivation, self-esteem, and a coherent view of the future. Those who talk, even facetiously, about becoming hookers and street hoods may have given up their search for an acceptable adult identity.

My most recent success with photography has been with Nicole D., a highly competent 14-year-old from the junior high school. She is one of the very few students I have encountered who has both recognized and exploited the fact that special education can provide a unique opportunity to receive intensive personal instruction in any subject one desires. As a special educator, I am so battered by opposition that when a student says, "Teach me," I will drop everything to oblige.

Nicole's mood fluctuates between eruptive and depressed. Often when she shows up for class she will look miserable and glower at the floor in sullen anger. Thirty-five minutes later she will emerge from the darkroom with six to eight decent prints to show for her time. Evidently she finds something regenerative in the darkroom procedures. Although she is young to seize on a career goal, she is very receptive to instruction about photographic theory. Once a week I see her for purely theoretical work, and as I take the book down from the shelf she smiles and says, "Daguerre, Paris, 1839," which happens to be the birth of photography and the first fact in her book. A year later she graduated from junior high to the high school and the chance to work with her individually was no longer available, either in her schedule or in mine. Her experiences with photography are now on their way to becoming a recreational episode. Nicole is now caught up in the customary round of language arts, social studies, and math while this area of former competence is slipping away from her.

Joy R., a third photography student, is truly talented. She had already attracted the attention of the art teacher and painted a mural that was on display in the administration building. Her intellectual abilities are among the best in the school, and she learned the essentials of darkroom technique with ease. She turned out to be the only student who really mastered the refinements of controlling contrast with graded filters.

To watch Joy take pictures of people was always a pleasure. She would involve herself fully in the process, taking pains to bring forth the best in her subjects. I find this particularly impressive, as adolescents tend to be narcissistic and self-absorbed. The art of making someone else look good is not something they would normally take to. Joy, however, will have her subjects turn their head to one side or another, she will coax a smile, and she has a perfect sense of timing, always getting the photograph at the moment of peak interest.

I praised her work constantly, which she had great difficulty accepting. She and her peers tend to interpret praise as signifying that the job was not really worth doing. Nevertheless, I was able to get Joy into a one-on-one tutorial and obtain approval for her to work alone in the darkroom.

And this was the point at which I began to lose her. She was assigned to the darkroom fourth period, and I would have to intercept her at the end of the third period and escort her to the darkroom. If I did not, she would take advantage of fourth period as a break and drift out of program. I would also have to give her a specific batch of negatives to work from and tell her what size prints to make. Otherwise there was a good chance that, even if she did make it as far as the darkroom, she would spend the period doing nothing. At the end of the period she would then reproach me for not having given her an assignment, even though the darkroom was full of negatives waiting to be printed.

In the absence of the usual supports she would simply fail to perform. For reasons I could not have anticipated she could not sustain her interest, she did not take pleasure in her mastery of the medium, and she did not yet view the subject as something that could become a part of her adult life. Here again the student's uncertain self-esteem and sense of the future got in the way. I still have hopes, however, of taking Joy out of her regular schedule for one period a day so that she can make a yearbook for the high school. When you least expect it, your efforts may suddenly clarify a student's sense of purpose and competence.

There have been some rewarding incidents in another subject area. A number of students had asked me about instruction in computer programming. I brought this to the attention of the principal who, as usual, was willing to say yes to anything within reason. When I brought my first programming student into the computer room for instruction, I had him copy a ten-line routine from a book on simple graphic displays. By means of a continuous loop the computer flashed stars and dashes on the screen creating the illusion of a rotating barber pole. The student copied the program from the book, made the inevitable keyboard errors, debugged the program, and then ran it. When the screen displayed the desired result, he leaped from his chair, grabbed my hand and shook it, and then made all his fellow students get up from their consoles and come over to see his achievement.

Although the students do a lot of work on computers, there was a significant difference here. Their usual computer work takes place in a passive or responsive situation: the screen will prompt them to answer questions about mathematics, history, language arts, geography, etc. When the answer is correct they hear a victorious trill of beeps and a congratulatory message appears on the screen, while an incorrect answer produces a strident blooper sound accompanied by a message on the screen wishing better luck next time. A student who programs on the computer, however, has turned the tables and forced the machine to do his bidding. Although they do not immediately grasp the procedures at work, they do realize that what appears on the screen, where it appears, and how long it stays there all lie within their control.

Another rewarding computer incident occurred with Nick P. He had been truant so much over the years that his education appeared to be permanently arrested at a sixth-grade level. He had asked for computer programming and, after entering a few shorter programs, embarked on five pages of programming that produced a rather elaborate word game. On the face of it, this work is little more than typing practice. One enters line after line of programming instructions which eventually become a complex network of branching and interlocking instructions performing elaborate operations.

Nick found a program that appealed to him, then sat down and spent over two hours working uninterruptedly at his terminal. And he came back and did the same on the two following days. Prior to this I had never seen him work at anything for more than ten minutes. Now, however, he was completely in the thrall of doing a novel piece of work. I was still apprehensive as to what the outcome would be, as there are always the typing errors to correct. Since the smallest error in program entry—even a comma in place of a colon—will cause a program to abort, there is inevitably a considerable amount of debugging to be done. Moreover, these students have little patience with being corrected, or with finding their errors and redoing slipshod work. To my surprise, he spent another two hours trying to run the program, locating faulty entries, and correcting them.

After finishing the program, however, Nick stopped coming around and went back to his truant ways. Although he had truly transcended his limitations for about a week, I was unable to engage him in this manner again. Moreover, since the programming was not part of his regular course load, there was a convenient escape hatch: he could go back to his regular schedule. I tried to get him to enter another game program, but that too he refused. The first program had been sufficient for his need to prove himself. At least in his own terms he had become an expert and there was nothing else I could tell him. Here again there was work to be done in terms of building self-regard and a sense of competence.

Finally, after two years at Leake & Watts, I finally found a student who was ready to take on programming in all its complexity. Darryl V. is assigned to me for one period a day and when I offered to teach him about computer operations, he was quick to take up my offer. We started off just as one would teach programming in an optimal school situation. I would have him copy simple routines from a book, run them, and then explain to me exactly what was happening. I would then sit down at his console and scramble the program so that it would not run and then tell him to debug it. After that I was able to get him to alter the program output. If, for example, his program produced a square on the screen with horizontal bands running through it, I could tell him to make it into a rectangle with vertical bands.

All of this he did not just patiently, but avidly. He is in fact the only student I have ever had at Leake & Watts whom I had to escort from his desk and out of the class at the end of the period— so great was his fascination with the subject at hand.

What's the catch? The catch is that Darryl belongs to that 10 or 15 percent of our population that is more psychotic than conduct-disordered. Unlike the great majority of students at Leake & Watts, who have responded to poor nurture by becoming oppositional and unmanageable, Darryl did not present any of these problems. He is a sensitive and intelligent young man with a history of auditory hallucinations but no trouble with teachers. My attempts to teach him were not immediately met by opposition or wild behavior. Darryl may have an uncertain grasp on reality, but in all the ways that enable education, he has internalized the restraints and self-control that make a person teachable. More important, however, he talks constantly about the career he hopes to make as a computer programmer. He is engaged in an age-appropriate attempt to reach out for a career, and he has the self-confidence to believe that he can actualize his hopes.

He has grasped the fact that today's work becomes tomorrow's competence. And, most important, he has not diverted education into behavior control. At present Darryl is progressing rapidly toward a real knowledge of the field. He is clearly excited about completing the program he is now keying in and is already asking questions about the various sub-routines that make it all work. He holds a very special position in my life, as there are many days on which my work with him is the only actual teaching I do. In special education, 30 minutes of demonstrable success a day is an indispensable tonic to my often failing energy and conviction.

Only with Darryl did I ever have what is one of the most important experiences in a student-teacher relationship: getting caught in a mistake. Occasionally I will glance over his shoulder while he is keying something in and inform him, "That's not going to work."

Darryl will turn around with a condescending smile on his face and point out some broader aspect of the program I had failed to notice. His usual remark on such occasions is, "Getting old, aren't you, Howe?" There is probably nothing more immediately encouraging for a student than being able to correct a teacher—assuming that it does not happen all the time!—as this is the promise that the younger generation will succeed the older.

Both photography and computer programming have on occasion been reasonably successful subjects. As fields of study they have two major features in common. First, they are immediately self-validating. If one makes a mistake with a computer program, it will fail to run and an error message will appear on the screen. Nothing is subject to interpretation and, when a student is set right by the computer screen, it does not carry the same odor of disgrace as having a school teacher criticize one's work.

With photography, too, the technique must be meticulous and consistent throughout. If something is botched somewhere along the way, this will be evident as a defect on the finished product. When there are finger prints or smudges on a photograph, there is no need for me to say anything. The problem is self-evident.

Everything that happens in the darkroom is so rigorously determined by the chemistry that the main thing one is teaching them is how to be careful. The more artistic aspects, such as tonal control and composition, depend on natural talent, and in this regard my students are exactly like other students—some have it and some do not.

In darkroom work one can have these students working at a decent level of proficiency in a brief time. They have the satisfaction of doing real work with visible results, using skills that have not been neglected or undermined by their fragmentary schooling.

Both photography and computer programming are based on new skills that have little association with previous failures. Particularly in the area of computer programming and data entry, much can be done for these students. To write one's first program is to step into an entirely new field of knowledge. It is neither strictly math nor language—it is a unique mode of symbolic thought that is accessible, at least on the entry level, even to those with sixth-grade math and language skills.

It has the further advantage of leading to possible white-collar employment. We have come a long way, but not all the way, since Malcolm X said to his junior high school teacher that he wanted to be a lawyer and was told to remember his place and consider carpentry. What is needed, especially in a school for troubled children whose academic skills are in arrears, is a vocational curriculum that has the potential of leading beyond menial employment.

Another field that appears to be rewarding for these students is small electronics. This is still relatively new for me, but I have had students assemble battery testers, Ohm meters, and oscillator circuits. Anything that is concrete and tangible will get their attention almost at once. This is somewhat like computer programming in that soldering resistors and capacitors into place is similar to keying in programs from a book. It is basically an exercise in manual dexterity that is devoid of abstract or conceptual content.

The first project I undertook was with two students, each of whom assembled code oscillators. Both are at the higher end of academic competence at our school, and they both exhibited a certain amount of male pride in knowing how things work. Roy P.

was our only male graduate last year and Lester D. was so competent that he was sent off to an outside school. My only difficulty
was in getting them to consider the theoretical aspects of what they
were doing. Once the devices were assembled, I tried to get them
to go through the circuit diagram and tell me what was happening.
After I had done my best to explain to them what resistors and
capacitors do, I asked them how it all worked. The explanation I
received as approximately as follows: "The electricity goes from the
battery through these resistors, and then you turn the volume knob
and push the key, and it makes a sound."

I could not get them to measure the voltage at various points
in the circuit, I could not get them to measure the impedance of
the resistors, I could not get them to ascertain where the current
switched from AC to DC. The fact that they had put it together
and that it worked was an adequate demonstration of their expertise. The experience was exactly the same as the one I had with the
students who were keying in game programs on the computer:
having done the concrete work, they felt the expertise was established. What I need to do now is determine the point at which my
students know enough to get the job done. Beyond this there really
is no need to vex them.

But in fact not all of my students have been averse to the
theoretical aspects of a project. I was caught by surprise by Sandi
G., one of the girls in my core group. She asked if she could do
electronics, and I promptly answered, "No, you can't, because I
can't get anyone to take the time to figure out what is really
happening."

This was a foil, and she knew it. "Come on, Howe. I really
want to try this. I'll learn the stuff you want." This was of course
all I needed to hear, so I took her on and she proceeded to do all
the things my previous students had failed to do. Sandi happens to
have serious reading problems and as a result has come to rely very
heavily on her memory. For example she will memorize bus and
subway routes, as she has difficulty in making sense of the charts
and maps. As with many learning impaired students, however, she
strives to compensate in other areas. She has the best memory of
all the students in my class for spoken information and also retains
information longer than the others. Her defense against her chaotic perception of things is to impose as much structure and coherence as possible on the information she can process.

Not knowing what to expect, I asked Sandi to analyze the

operation of her first project. She found the logic of the device both comprehensible and interesting. If the voltage dropped from nine volts to a volt-and-a-half, she knew she had to look for some kind of resistor. If there was a switching operation involving a lower voltage and a higher voltage, she would look for a transistor and even be able to identify the leads on the transistor. Here again a door had opened on an area of potential competence. Unfortunately, once again there was not sufficient latitude in the academic program for me to be able to pursue this subject with her.

I find that electronics occupies a middle ground between photography and computer programming. At the level of building and trouble-shooting small circuits it is both manual and conceptual. The soldering, like darkroom work, requires a fine touch and attention to detail, while the circuitry requires a grasp of mathematical and electronic concepts.

Another area where computers have made a difference is getting the students to write. I am always interested in what they will have to say, but often find it difficult to get anything out of them. These are students who take no joy in writing, and to put something on paper is to undergo a tiresome and threatening ordeal. They feel inhibited by their faltering and inadequate grasp of written language. They must ask for assistance in spelling and they are often at a loss for words. And if they get past all of these obstacles, they still feel alienated by the formal nature of written expression. When I ask them to write about themselves they feel further constrained by their many disagreeable recollections of social workers, therapists, and psychiatrists asking them how they feel, what they want, what went wrong, and why they do the things they do.

The experience of writing into a computer does much to break down this resistance. There is something about composing onto a screen that is more like playing an arcade game than writing. The screen image lacks the documentary permanence of something that has been worked out on paper—it has a transient and spectral quality, and can be made to disappear with a key stroke. Thus, my students can be induced to impart to the computer the reflections and experiences that they refuse to put on paper.

Computer writing has another advantage—the ease with which I can get my students to correct their work. Because of the element of play in working on a computer I have been able to scribble all over a printout with a red pencil and hand it back to the student. Making corrections is just another video game involving horizontal and vertical movements of the cursor. The fact that their composition is still a fluid entity, drifting about on the screen, means that corrections take place without defacing a finished piece of work.

There is in this something of the little child writing a letter to Santa. My students will write to parents or siblings they have not seen in years and whose whereabouts are unknown. They will write pained and laconic statements about how their lives went wrong and what could make things better again. The writing has been a self-sufficient act of reverie that requires no external confirmation. When they occasionally do ask for a printout, they will read it with expectant curiosity, as though it were the work of a different person. Out of respect for their privacy I will ask if they mind whether I save their file to a disk, and they rarely object. Once the words disappear from the screen, they cease to exist and the feelings that gave rise to them once again slip below the surface. Although writing is only a small part of the overall academic agenda, it is a task that can be greatly lightened by enlisting the computer.

When it comes to teaching traditional academic subject matter, the job is difficult no matter how one attacks it. I have found, however, that there is no substitute for standing up in front of the class and presenting the material forcefully, personally, and unremittingly. It is clear to me that these students remember almost nothing of their "quiet seat work." All the workbooks, handouts, and dittos are simply an academic recreation that keeps them in their chairs until the end of the period. Although teachers may prefer not to reflect on this, students are distinctly aware of it. When they hurl their work on the floor and exclaim, "This is bull shit," they are not just being oppositional; they are passing judgment on the quality of their education.

This year, in response to being left without a teaching aide for a month, I resorted to standing up in front of the class and actually instructing them. Quiet seat work is a possibility only when the students can receive prompt assistance if they become stuck or distracted. When there is a wild group, some of whom are functioning at a level of marginal literacy, this is a full-time job for at least two people.

Out of desperation I resorted to active instruction. Even under the best of conditions this is extremely difficult: the children resist having someone speak to them for any length of time and it takes tremendous energy and animation to hold their attention.

Once I started doing this, however, it took about three weeks for it to become apparent that they greatly preferred it to quiet seat work. Every four or five days I give them a test on the material covered and they take great pleasure in proving to me and to themselves that they have absorbed new information.

They will now take copies of earlier tests to students from other classes and see how they do. When another student does not know what the white blood cells do or the significance of the 5th Amendment, my students are jubilant—so much so that they recently made up a card for me in the computer room saying, "Thank you for teaching us."

I rarely have an opportunity to test my assumptions. Recently one of our alumni, Barry B., who had left a year ago, came back to pay us a call, and confirmed my feeling that the students appreciate instruction. He happened to arrive during my prep period, so I was the only teacher who had time for him. Barry is a criminalized young man, and the outcome of that story is far from told, but like many such students he is brighter and more competent than the average. He is now going to a New York City public school for children at risk, and I asked him how he is doing. He is taking real academic courses with real academic content, and it is a struggle. He said he was having a hard time of it, but went on to say, "Thank God for Miss K. and Mr. M. They were the only ones around here doing any teaching. All the rest was just bull shit."

It is so seldom that we have a chance to evaluate what we are doing that I was thrilled to pass on this report to K and M. Like everyone else in this business, they are beset by doubts whether anything is ever getting done. It was a bracing experience to have Barry come back from the outside world and tell his teachers that there is no substitute for teaching.

Something else that works—and it is almost too pedestrian to point out—is the cumulative impact of the teacher's presence. When a child and a teacher are thrown together for an extended period—say, two hours a day for five months—the child will begin to do what the teacher wants. This is not the triumph of compliance and docility; it happens because a teacher's wishes and intentions will finally force their way into manifestation. The cumulative force of a teacher saying, "Sit still and do your work," or "Open your book and give your education a chance" is real and discernible. The teacher whose primary concern is control and behavior will find by mid-year that progress has been made. Likewise, the teacher who gives her primary energies to instruction will find that after several months her students are starting to learn.

Whether one chooses instruction or behavior control as the primary agenda, there is a price to be paid either way. The teacher whose foremost concern is behavior control will not get the academic results that straight teaching elicits. And the teacher who is narrowly focused on instruction will have a somewhat more rowdy class.

I was able to put these suppositions to the test two years ago when I compared the reading tests of all students over the duration of a school year. Twice a year—early in the fall and late in the spring—we administer a standardized test to determine the reading level of all students in the school, basically as a means of taking our own pulse. Without exception the classes that were run on a stricter regimen experienced lower overall average gains in reading proficiency than those classes that were looser and more permissive. Although the students in the stricter classes had doubtless spent more "busy time" than the others, this activity had been stultifying rather than liberating. I have done this calculation only once and with a base of about forty students. Another couple of years will tell whether there is a viable approach to effective pedagogy to be found in these numbers.

As I try to make sense of these experiences and come up with practical and predictable strategies, a few basic facts emerge. If a child has low self-esteem and no acceptable concept of her adult life, the first order of business should not be the "remediation of deficits." It should be something productive and rewarding that will propel the child toward significant competence. Ideally, such a curriculum will emphasize those skills in which the student has some hope of doing well. Then the remedial work can ride on the ensuing swell of confidence and motivation. When it comes to what happens in the classroom, I would give priority to teaching over behavior management, on the assumption that forceful teaching will generally cause behavior to stabilize at an acceptable level.

7

The Downward Spiral

In 1831 the Leake & Watts Childrens Home was founded as the legacy of high-minded and prosperous New Yorkers. In the decade from 1820 to 1830, private philanthropy took an active interest in providing relief for orphans and the hapless offspring of destitute mothers. Formerly detained in alms houses along with adult vagrants, drunks, and petty criminals, these children needed a setting that could provide a better semblance of home life. The righteous and optimistic philanthropists of the early nineteenth century took it upon themselves to educate unfortunate children in the habits of discipline and industry that would ensure for them a productive role in society. The project was animated by a sense of duty and spiritual vocation that is expressed in this entry from the Leake & Watts Visitors' Book from the year 1845:

> The gratification always attendant on visits of this kind has in no wise been lessened by repeated calls here. Order has been everywhere apparent while the religious and intellectual culture of the orphan children here gathered will compare favorably with any similar institution that I have ever visited. That

105

God in his mercy may reward those interested in maintaining this noble enterprise and watch over and guard the young immortals is the sincere prayer of

(Signed)

In the century-and-a-half since this was written, our major cities have become a monstrous and unmanageable aggregate of social inequality, and they are populated by a gravely disenfranchised underclass that lacks employment, appropriate schooling, opportunity for advancement and, above all, hope. In the helping services, as in all other areas, the sweetness and light of the nineteenth century has been rendered mute and impotent by the developments of the twentieth century. What would be the prayer of a nineteen-century visitor on behalf of the young man who wrote this autobiography in my class two years ago?

My story is this. It all started when I was eleven years old. I was living in Coney Island. No, not in no fuck-up weakass Marlboro Project, but between Surf and Mermaid Avenues. I was small and really didn't know how to fight. So one day people that I knew made up a crew name the Forty Thieves. I was given the name Crime. I used to snatch chains, steal pocketbooks, grocery money, and stick people. These things were the move.

So one day last year I moved to Bed Stuy (do or die) and I met this kid name Pistol Pop. We would go around sticking up crack spots until one day on the 24th of December my home boy was killed. He was tortured. Whoever did it, did it like this. They knocked out all his teeth, stuck the fat end of a baseball bat up his asshole. He was raped and then to end this fucking shit they shot him in the fucking head.

Now I swear to the dead Father Allah, if I find who did it, I am going to put two bullets in his head. But anyway I cooled down. Now I'm just chillin.

The inescapable fact that now confronts the worker at Leake & Watts is this: When incidents of this sort become legion, there is no social-service intervention that will rectify the problem, restore the family, and reeducate the youth. Until the devastating conditions behind such lives have been radically altered, any response is no more than a palliative.

A teacher tries to maintain at least a spark of hope that his exertions will endure and bear fruit, and yet I find myself weighing the net gain for a student who has learned to multiply decimals against the chaos of the world that produced him. At such times I find that my achievements in "this noble enterprise," as the nineteenth-century visitor referred to Leake & Watts, are intolerably paltry.

What was happening at Leake & Watts 150 years ago, when both the problem and the remedy seemed to lie within manageable bounds? Although the personal histories of the early residents are not available, there is sufficient material to disclose both the agenda and the expectations. Here is an entry from the Punishment Book for 1844:

> ——— was slightly corrected by the teacher in evening school and became very insolent, was ordered to take off his jacket (for a beating) and refused. But was promptly corrected with more severity, made to obey unconditionally by the teacher.

Although I do not envy the license with which teachers beat their charges, nor do I regard breaking a child's will to be a particularly estimable goal, I cannot fail to recognize that there were expectations, interventions, and results. To be able to identify insolence as something undesirable, to take measures against it and, for the moment at least, to put it to rest describes people doing real work under viable conditions.

There can be no doubt that the sheer oppositional will of the children 150 years ago was of a very different order from what we encounter now. Here is an incident from 1853 involving an egregious rowdy, recorded in the handwriting of the director himself:

> ——— went to the city without permission to his uncle and returned in the afternoon. As he seemed perfectly indifferent about it, I confined him, intending to keep him a day or two in confinement and then release him if he could be sorry. He was quite insolent, however, and amused himself by singing, dancing, sitting with his legs out the window and calling out to the boys underneath. This afternoon immediately on my return from the city I heard him while I was in my office, hollering to some of the boys and, on looking out, I perceived that he was throwing down parts of the several New Testaments that were in the room for perusal. I went to the room

to punish him for his flagrant misconduct. Being a large strong boy of a badly governed temper, he refused to be corrected, and endeavoring to force the rattan (whip) from me. I was therefore obliged to treat him with some severity. During this punishment he shouted to the extent of his voice and was heard in all parts of the house.

All this beating and shouting is of course primitive by today's standards of child care, and the presence of the New Testament in the discipline room now seems quaint and archaic. As late as 1936, however, each graduate of Leake & Watts received a Bible with his or her name embossed on it. And when child-care methods became more lenient, Leake & Watts followed the trend and continued to turn out competent alumni. In 1917 when the Board of Trustees forbade all corporal punishment, solitary confinement, and loss of meals, Leake & Watts successfully applied loving solicitude in a simulated home environment.

In the late 1920s and early 1930s, Leake & Watts graduates were captains of both the football and basketball teams at Columbia University. Colgate College was the school of choice and a steady trickle of Leake & Watts graduates went there. The boys' band was so good it was in demand for outside functions and the basketball team could beat the West Point plebes. A Leake & Watts Alumni Association was founded in 1884, and until 1957 it continued to hold meetings, collect dues, keep minutes, and stage social functions.

In a taped testimonial from a Leake & Watts resident from the years 1923 to 1936, the man recalled above all else a cottage parent, formerly a British Army nurse, who had lavished upon him a degree of loving concern that remained an inspiration for the rest of his life. He recalls with dry humor how strict his teachers had been and confesses that in his young mind he could not quite grasp what they were trying to do. He then pauses before adding that even in old age he is not quite sure what their purpose had been.

The children at Leake & Watts continued to be teachable and competent right through the 1940s. There is a plaque in our administration building with the names of graduates who gave their lives for their country during World War II. There is a similar memorial for World War I, but there is nothing for the Korean War or the Vietnam War. During my four years at Leake & Watts only two of our graduates have been accepted for the military.

Many more would have been admitted, had they met the qualifications. In the postwar years, however, Leake & Watts had been drifting away from its original task of providing a home for competent children without family or guardians.

A regular occurrence in the history of child care is that the institutionalization of competent children falls into popular discredit. This happened in 1914, at which time Leake & Watts was forced to discharge all the children, only to bring them back a year later. During the 1930s and 1940s the conventional wisdom began to move once again toward the view that competent children are best served by adoption or foster care. The line of reasoning behind this is entirely sensible: institutional care is too impersonal, it allows too much opportunity for abuse, and it cannot recreate the nuclear structure of the child-parent relationship.

As a result, many of the orphan-care institutions were forced out of business during the 1940s and 1950s. It was recognized, however, that some children were simply too unmanageable to be good candidates for normal family living. Even the most patient and saintly foster parents could find themselves in over their heads if entrusted with a wild and delinquent child. These are the conditions that gave rise to the Residential Treatment Center. In such a facility there would be a highly structured program, a tight disciplinary regimen, and clinical staff capable of providing psychotherapy and, when necessary, psychotropic drugs.

Leake & Watts became a Residential Treatment Center (RTC) in 1977. This means that the current criterion for admission is that the child has proven to be too oppositional and difficult for placement in an extended family, in foster care, or in a group home. The rise of the RTC acknowledged the existence of a growing number of children for whom nurture and family life had been so radically defective that they could be contained only in a highly specialized environment.

The RTC is a facility for children who have a chaotic home life and symptoms that do not respond well to conventional therapy. The mode of treatment is one of complete immersion in a well-regulated and nurturing environment. The goal is to build up the child's ego to the point where he or she can negotiate a more conventional environment along with age-appropriate challenges.

Two salient characteristics of the children now at Leake & Watts are a chaotic home situation and an inability to respond to conventional therapy. If there is a parent on the scene, that parent is apt to be psychotic, drug-involved, given to violence, negligent, or criminalized. Referral is based on the realization that, painful and traumatic as it may be to remove a child from the home, there are conditions where this can be preferable to staying put.

Moreover, the child who has been reared under chaotic or deprived conditions is not a good candidate for conventional therapy. A child who is trusting of adults and able to verbalize problems could conceivably stay in a troubled home and could, through therapy, learn how to take things in stride. Thus the children now at Leake & Watts do not have a satisfactory home and are too hurt and angry for the introspection that enables therapy.

As for the mode of treatment, if the child cannot benefit from intensive personal treatment with a therapist, then the entire setting must be made therapeutic. The term for this is "milieu therapy," which implies that everything—making your bed, attending school, playing softball, doing cottage chores, observing rules—is a form of therapy. The assumption is that such a setting will strengthen the child who has an uncontrolled id and a weak ego. The hope is that children who lack the ability to engage in treatment on an interpersonal and emotional level will benefit from a structured and nurturing environment.

This means that all persons who come together with these children, from the cooks to the teachers to the cottage staff, are therapists in the full sense of the word. Their exchanges and interactions with the children are the therapy itself and are charged with all the transference, countertransference, and emotional weight that characterizes therapy.

Since building up the ego is one of the primary goals of an RTC, the school becomes one of the most important forces in a resident's life. Because of the specialized nature of the teaching, an RTC such as Leake & Watts will tend to have its own school, as the teachers are engaged in the rather specialized business of getting undermotivated students to exploit their potential—wherever it can be found—to the fullest possible extent.

Thirty-five years ago the treatment goal of the RTC was somewhat obscure, and this is still the case today. The original hope, at least on the part of the clinicians, was that a well-regulated setting would build sufficient ego strength and trust in adults to enable therapy. The child could then be moved from the RTC either to his own home or to a group home and get to the source of his problems through therapy.

There was also the possibility, at least in theory, that the child would not necessarily become responsive to therapy, but through improved self-esteem and the influence of a structured environment, would become competent to move to a group home and more challenging demands. In this case the underlying problems would still exist, but there would have been a viable adjustment.

At this point the potential weaknesses of the RTC concept emerge. It has never been determined how long this process of building a viable ego should take. (At present we like to think in terms of two years.) Moreover, what is to be done with the resident who does not appear to be moving toward enhanced ego strength and some measure of trust in adults? Are there some children for whom this goal is possible, if not after two years then perhaps after six years? Are there indeed some children for whom this goal can never be achieved? What is to be their fate? These questions are as vexing today as they were when the RTC concept was first introduced.

An essential ingredient of the initial RTC concept was the realization that the treatment extends to the post-institutional placement of the child. If you remove a child from a chaotic home situation, give him his first experience of real competence, and then send him back to a chaotic situation, you will undo your own work. The problems with which an RTC concerns itself are not resolved until the incompetent child becomes the competent adult.

There are some implicit difficulties in the RTC concept that can run out of control. It is one thing to accept the premise that a certain type of child is too undersocialized for foster care or a group home; to bring 80 to 100 such children together into a single residential facility, however, gives rise to an incredibly concentrated and potent surge of opposition, maladjustment, and anger. And indeed for much of the day, the sole agenda is chaos containment.

Once these children have been brought together in an RTC, there is an immediate need for a highly specialized form of therapy, the exact nature of which is far from clear. In its original conception the RTC was a finely tuned healing institution in which all staff skillfully collaborated to mend and rebuild the lives of the residents. Because of the sheer difficulty of the situation and the financial constraints under which public assistance programs work, what was originally intended as significant treatment has lost much

of its therapeutic conviction and drifted in the direction of custodial care.

The present task of Leake & Watts is now vastly more difficult
than anyone could have imagined 50 years ago. There are changes
that have crept up on us without anyone really taking stock of what
the cumulative effect would be.

First and most important, the term of treatment has been
drastically reduced. For the children admitted in 1903 the average
stay was 8 years; the longest was 14 years and the shortest was 3.
As I write this, there is a movement afoot to set 2 years as the
absolute limit and to keep no one past the age of 18. It is reasoned
that two years should be sufficient for the RTC treatment mode to
have taken effect, and if this has not been the case, then the child
was not a good candidate in the first place.

An obvious and inevitable consequence of long-term residence is going to be a more powerful and intensive commitment to
the growth and welfare of the child. The longer you keep a child,
the more you are forced to recognize the results of your efforts.
Thus if you keep a child for a mere two years, you can set short-
term compliance as your goal. Whether the child has developed
new strength and competence can be left to be discovered further
on down the road.

On the other hand, if you have a child with you for eight
years, you will come to a very full knowledge of how well you are
doing. There can be a couple of years of short-term compliance,
while the child remains broken and incomplete within. Continued
impairment will make itself known, and when this happens one is
forced to rethink the initial agenda along lines that optimize continuous and progressive growth. For the institution that offers long-
term residence, there is no other place for the buck to stop.

The orphans of the nineteenth century, and today's conduct-
disordered children, have the same basic problem—discontinuous
and inadequate family life. This means that they have a common
need for the intensive and sustained attention of competent and
concerned adults. Thus, the traditional agenda at Leake & Watts,
well into this century, has been to make up for this deficit and embrace the lives of the children as fully as possible. The unequivocal
goal was to send them forth as competent and autonomous adults.

The fact that Leake & Watts does not now offer long-term
care for children of course is not a deliberate choice to provide

inferior treatment, but the inevitable consequence of being an RTC. This treatment is, by definition, short-term. I fear that in the minds of the initial framers of the RTC concept there may have been an unspeakable realization behind this policy: that the RTC candidate is too damaged to respond meaningfully to any treatment, long-term or short-term.

Once the short-term treatment becomes established, unintended harmful consequences arise further on down the road. Since the treatment is already no more than a segment in the history of the child, we seek to make a virtue of a vice and justify further segmentation. Within the school there is an ongoing debate: should the students be assigned to a core teacher who is with them throughout the day, or should they move from class to class with a different teacher for each subject? The argument in favor of moving them around is that they must soon learn to accommodate a variety of styles and personalities.

Each phase of their lives then comes under the supervision of a different specialist. There is the social worker who, at least before the law, functions *in loco parentis*. Then there are the residential staff, recreation staff, clinical staff, and education staff. Under optimum conditions these people all get together once every three months to compare notes and see if they can create a composite picture of the child's progress.

Another unspoken consideration probably weighs against intensive staff exposure: the more involved these children become with one person, the more liberty they feel to express the pain and anger that have filled their lives. This can take the form of explosive behavior, depressed withdrawal, or high-spirited mischief. An RTC responds to this by running the children through a perfunctory sequence of activities where they are expected to give at least nominal compliance to the presiding adult.

On the other hand, if one chooses to work against segmentation and assign them to fewer staff for longer periods of time, one can maintain the expectation that they will relieve themselves of some of the emotional baggage they are carrying about. This approach is supported by the theory that a healthy child will act up at home and be an angel on the outside. The RTC mode is to create an environment where everything is "outside" and the children are expected to behave like angels all the time. If, however, there is no home in which to explore the need to act out, then bad behavior may begin to seek other more circuitous and harmful avenues of expression.

The intensity of personal involvement is further diluted by the fact that there are no longer cottage parents. In earlier times each of the children's cottages was staffed by a resident couple who presided over meals, chores, rising in the morning, and retiring at the end of the day; they mended clothes, and saw to all the little niceties of family life. Now the job is done by cottage staff who, like nurses in a hospital, come and go in eight-hour shifts.

The pragmatic reason for this is that these children in many ways are more like patients than like members of a family. They are so oppositional and emotionally impoverished that staff who would be willing and able to take on their lives in big chunks simply cannot be found. Such children make voracious demands for adult attention and they are very happy to receive even the negative attention that comes as a consequence of bad behavior. Although it can be stimulating and often rewarding to have inordinate demands made on one's energy, there is a dire price to pay in terms of sheer fatigue and depletion. This is a pervasive reality for people in this line of work and is well-known to those who run things. Thus we continue to break up the lives of these children into little pieces and then reassure ourselves that they need varied experiences.

Unfortunately the negative consequences of short-term and fragmented treatment are everywhere apparent. One of the most obvious is that the children are nowhere near ready to move on after a couple of years at Leake & Watts. Despite a fierce temper and a propensity for getting into dangerous fights, a girl who had been in the agency for three years gained the favorable attention of a number of people, particularly in the school where her superior intelligence was appreciated. But, as part of the "get-them-out-after-two-years" movement, she was told that she would be required to leave shortly. At the time it was remarked in her presence that it would be a good idea to get her out before she got into a fight where someone got hurt.

Within a month of this she got into exactly such a fight and, although she was the one who got hurt, the pressure is now greater than ever to get her out, as she has proven how dangerous she can be. It was clear, at least to those who knew her in the school, that the fight was a *cri de coeur* to let her stay. The agency had in fact achieved a considerable degree of success with this child in the sense that there were several adults with whom she felt connected; moreover, after the three most stable and productive years of her life, she was nowhere near ready at the age of 16 to be sent off to a new setting with a new cast of characters.

At such times it becomes apparent that although the buck stops briefly in my classroom, it really stops nowhere. When this girl arrives at her next placement, her habitual distrust of adult relationships will be renewed, and many of the gains she made at Leake & Watts will be dissipated by the pressures of accommodating herself to a new environment.

For the first 100 years of its existence Leake & Watts was essentially an instance of private philanthropy. Now it is a subcontractor to the city and state and subsists almost entirely on public funds. Social historians have observed that from about 1870 to 1920 America was engaged in a paramount effort to attain world-class capability in manufacture and production. The growth of industry, transportation, and urban centers of commerce followed by the depression left an incapacitated and impoverished underclass. The government began to take an active interest in social welfare, the consummation of which was the New Deal and the many social welfare programs of the 1930s. Behind these developments was the realization that the poor were too numerous and deprived to be effectively assisted by private philanthropy.

These changes had a profound impact on an organization such as Leake & Watts. In 1916 the city of New York was paying $2.50 a week toward the support of each child. Now the entire expense of maintaining the children, which is in excess of $35,000 per child per year, is carried entirely by public assistance programs. When a service is supported by public rather than private funds, the inevitable result is that the emphasis shifts from treatment to administrative compliance and organization. The public agencies that serve the deprived and disadvantaged dispense many millions of dollars and impose upon a Leake & Watts elaborate guidelines supported by detailed documentation. This consists mainly in recording every aspect of a child's status, treatment, testing, contacts outside the agency, evaluations, and family relations.

The social workers are the most oppressed and burnout-prone group at Leake & Watts. Of the 12 who were on staff when I started four years ago, only one is still around. The rest have left, either in exasperation or depression. When I ask a social worker what is the most debilitating aspect of the job, the answer is always the same: the crushing burden of paperwork. When I inquire further, I find that the general estimate is that 50 percent of their time goes into paperwork.

The state requires constant assurance that the residents at Leake & Watts continue to meet the criteria for placement in an RTC and that treatment continues to be in compliance with regulations. Unfortunately this is not a dynamic situation wherein the social worker is making potent interventions in the life of the child. Rather, it is a static situation wherein the social worker is constantly making sure that the status quo is appropriately documented. Each home visit is logged and recorded. Each conversation with a parent or guardian goes down in the annals. Although the ostensible purpose is to analyze and fine-tune treatment, the actual result is that correct and timely completion of paperwork turns out to be an end in itself.

It is disturbing to see the price that social workers pay for this situation. They generally comprise a compassionate group of individuals who have gone into the field to help other people. When they stumble into the child welfare system, they are often last seen sinking under a rising swell of papers. When they finally become demoralized and leave, this has a devastating effect on the morale of the children. In theory the social worker is the primary advocate and parent-substitute for a child. If there is a change every year or so, this has a destabilizing effect on the children, who have trouble enough availing themselves of adult help even when they can get to know the person over an extended period of time.

The travail of documentation is then compounded by the travail of compliance. The newest directives from the State Board of Education require that a student, irrespective of emotional stability or intellectual capacity, must be exposed to the specific subject matter appropriate to his or her grade. Thus if the 10th-grade requirement is for all students to know *Moby Dick*, there can be no substitutions or evasions. Those who can read the original will do so, while those with language skills on a third-grade level will see a video or read a comic book on *Moby Dick*. With many of our students, schooling is possibly only when the girls are separated from the boys, the readers from the nonreaders, the noisy defiant from the sullen defiant, and so on. If, however, we must lump together all the 10th-graders for the "Moby Dick experience," all our fine-tuning in terms of differential treatment and meeting individual needs takes a back seat to compliance.

Once the demands of the system have become permanently and deeply imbedded in a program, compliance itself becomes the primary objective. A good agency is one in which the social workers are up-to-date on their documentation, the school has a current education program for each student, the psychiatric evaluations are done at proper intervals, and the minutes of the most recent treatment conference are promptly typed and circulated. Beneath this flurry of well-modulated activity neither the system that establishes the guidelines nor the agency that carries them out can maintain a primary concern with the progress of the individual child.

What is needed is to look unflinchingly at what it will take to treat and enable these children. During the first 100 years of Leake & Watts, conduct-disorder and the RTC were unheard of. For the criminal offenders there was the house of refuge, which evolved into the reform school in this century. Of course there were antisocial and aggressive children, but no one had thought of rounding up the most unmanageable children and bringing them together for treatment in one facility.

The sheer emotional intensity generated by even small clusters of these children is so great that the staff can take it only in small doses. The children's greatest need is to be enveloped by the intensive and unfailing attention of a concerned adult. And yet the emotional needs of any one of these children could consume the energies of a full-time adult. As a result, there is a ceaseless quest for structured programs that will manage behaviors and improve socialization. Such programs are worthy and significant in that they impose structure and expectations on the general environment. They are not truly curative, however, in that they do not reach out to fill the emotional void in the lives of these children. When a program is compromised in this manner, there is always the likelihood that actual treatment has deteriorated into custodial care.

A further measure to shield the staff from overexposure is to segment their involvement with the children. In all fairness it must be said that the demands from the children are nothing less than devastating. Those who qualify for RTC treatment are so angry and recalcitrant that, as things are now constituted, only a changing cast of professionals can take the heat.

From where I sit in my classroom, I feel that I am stopping up a small hole in the dam. When I catch an occasional glimpse beyond my immediate post, I notice that the whole dam is rent with flaws and fissures. As the social services have become better funded and more aware of where to find the casualties, agencies like Leake & Watts have received a steady stream of undersocialized children. The first order of business is simply to find a safe place for them and take off the hard edge of their most egregious misconduct. This, however, is no more than the first step toward lasting and curative treatment.

Beyond this lies a larger problem that must be addressed if the work at Leake & Watts is to make sense. Can society do something to enable the minority underclass and bring it into the mainstream of our culture? Until there is a dynamic and effective resolution to this question, Leake & Watts will continue to flounder like a lifeboat that picks up survivors from a sinking ship, tells them they should look into learning how to swim, and then throws them overboard.

8

Windows of
Opportunity

On a day-to-day basis I find that I am overwhelmed by
the pain and chaos I encounter. There is a tendency among people
in human-service fields to feel that nothing short of a social rev-
olution and a radical reallocation of resources is going to make a
difference. To cling to this view, however, is to preclude the
possibility of change. Although this work is done under great pressure and extreme constraints of time, energy, and resources, I
believe there is much to be done that lies within our immediate
reach, particularly as regards our basic approach to residential treatment and special education.

The current concept behind residential treatment is vague,
dated, and inadequate. Our greatest shortcoming is an unwillingness to recognize how gravely disabled the children are who come
to us. The truth is that the problem of the children of Leake &
Watts has its roots in their family history going back for a couple
of generations, and is the outgrowth of the socioeconomic chaos of
the inner city. This situation is quite unlike anything in the earlier
history of Leake & Watts. Up until 40 years ago the resources and
employment opportunities in New York City were sufficient for any

given national or ethnic group to break out of extreme deprivation within a couple of generations.

It is one thing to assume, as Aichhorn did in the 1920s in Vienna, that a truant and oppositional child can be taken from an unstable family, receive treatment for a year or two, and then return home to shoulder his appropriate obligations. It is far different to resurrect the life of a child who has been in foster care since the age of six months, and has never known any significant nurturing. It is palpably and demonstrably erroneous to imagine that such a child can be sent to an RTC for a couple of years, be placed on a B-Mod system, and then sent out into society as a viable and productive adult. There are four areas, however, where the RTC could reevaluate its mode of operation and aim for concrete results: the goal of treatment, mode of treatment, term of treatment, and follow-up. It requires no innovative or revolutionary vision to come up with some suggestions. Since the late nineteenth century, dedicated and intelligent people have been thinking and writing about how to deal with undersocialized children. The answers are straightforward and obvious; the only difficulty is that it requires tremendous patience and determination to implement them.

The RTC concept, as originally developed, had a clearly clinical and therapeutic orientation. Aichhorn's approach was to engage the affective energies of the children to the point where they would be amenable to psychotherapy. Likewise the 1954 seminar sponsored by the American Orthopsychiatric Association saw the RTC as a structured and stable setting that would force undesirable attitudes and behaviors into retreat. Then the more verbal and self-aware children could enter into therapy while those less gifted in these areas would at least develop the ego strength to become viable adults.

Now, however, it is highly questionable whether the RTC population will ever respond to conventional therapy or even develop significant ego strength. Without taking full account of these limitations, we generally offer one of two possible goals: return to the family, or "graduate" to independent living in a group home. The two, however, can hardly be viewed as treatment goals; they are simply physical destinations that lie at the end of residential treatment. Once it is acknowledged that these children do not respond well to conventional therapy, then they really step beyond the reach of the clinician's arsenal. This was clear to the participants in the 1954 Ortho seminar, where the two greatest needs of these children were identified as building ego strength and developing trust in adults. Once these goals are posited, then one can deploy all the precision and methodology of the clinician to ascertain needs, measure progress, and propose the specific strategies for obtaining results.

If building ego strength and developing trust in adults are to be the purpose of treatment, then the mode of treatment will be to create an environment that serves this objective as fully as possible. This means that the children will be provided with as many opportunities as possible to enter into rewarding and productive relationships with adults. It means that the children will be assessed for their strengths and will be assigned activities that utilize these strengths. It means that they will be encouraged and assisted in identifying viable and respectable career goals. And the entire experience will be supported by ensuring that the new arrivals see their elder peers achieve these goals.

If adult relationships are to be of paramount importance, then steps must be taken to avoid fragmenting the children's personal experiences. Some activities will create companionate relationships between staff and the children. Social workers will have to be relieved of some of their clerical duties so they can be installed more fully into the lives of their charges. The treatment centers must acknowledge the therapeutic potential of the social workers and take effective measures to ensure that they like their work and want to stay put. At present the social workers are so badgered, busy, and demoralized that their charges have no real relationship with them other than hustling them for privileges and passes.

Once a resident has been assigned to a particular teacher, social worker, and cottage parent, a conscientious attempt should be made to keep all these figures in place for the duration of the child's stay. Under present conditions, whenever a child is moved from one cottage to another or is promoted in school, a new cast of caretakers is installed. The therapeutic team should comprise a tight unit whose place in a resident's life is consistent and clearly defined. The communication between staff members should be intensive, continuous, and highly visible to the children. There should be functions at which the cottage staff, teachers, and social workers are brought together with the children—meals, outings, birthday parties, movies.

Occasionally, circumstances will throw me together in class

with the same student for two years running. The difference between one and two years is enormous: the additional year leads to
a deeper and more durable bond, which then becomes a source of
growth, compliance, and productive work. Conversely, students
are always being switched to new teachers and then drifting out of
my reach just as we come to the verge of new possibilities.

The therapeutic team should be informed in depth about the
problems, histories, and treatment goals of their charges. There
should be monthly treatment conferences in which each team
member would be assigned a short-term goal with the child and
held accountable at the next team meeting. The team members
would be drawn into a tight circle of concern for the children and
they would monitor their progress closely.

This would constitute the real therapy in the lives of the
students, and it would be acknowledged as such. Even as things are
constituted now, the staff who are with the children on a continuous and intensive basis already are therapists in all the salient
senses of the term. Let them get the training, support, and recognition that go with doing such sensitive and demanding work.

In the concept of "milieu therapy," we fail to acknowledge
how damaged these children are. Effective treatment requires more
than a tightly structured environment. It requires a staff that fully
grasps the condition of the children, how they became what they
are, and what the prospects are for helping them. Members of the
therapy team should possess a common body of knowledge on the
cause, treatment, and likely prognosis for conduct-disorder.

The treatment of conduct-disordered children has become
disreputable in psychiatric circles, and perhaps psychiatrists can
afford to take this position, but society as a whole cannot. If these
children do not receive effective treatment during adolescence,
they become an ever-more-costly burden either in the penal system
or on the welfare rolls. The sheer magnitude of the problem, and
the potential expense to the taxpayer, should be inducement
enough for a results-oriented approach to the conduct-disordered
child.

To make the treatment more effective, a more precise differential evaluation is needed than is now available. Under the general heading of residential treatment we round up a wide variety of
children into a motley heap and recommend a single course of
treatment: a structured environment with clear expectations supported by a swift and efficient system of reward and punishment.

This is viewed as a broad umbrella that can envelop the child who has been abused and neglected since birth along with the one who has become truant within the last year because of drug use, as well as the one who is newly arrived from Jamaica and has not adjusted to the city. As the system now functions, an agency like Leake & Watts receives a broad spectrum of children. At one end there are the radically criminalized children who bide their time with us for a couple of years before fulfilling what they have always known would be their destiny—going to prison. At the other end are those who have recently experienced some family chaos and are undergoing temporary adjustment problems. Since the system is not serious about enabling these children, it does not take the trouble to fine-tune its exertions and single out those who have a good chance of overcoming their weaknesses.

Even as things are now constituted, we have some measure of success with perhaps 20 percent of the children. These are the ones who complete a high school diploma, are not engaged in criminal activity when last seen, and are able to hold a low-level, part-time job off grounds for a couple of months. The rudiments for a treatment program for the conduct-disordered would start with an analysis of what these children have in common in terms of family history, admitting diagnosis, and general cognitive functioning. In my own experience, the more proficient children tend to have in common a relatively stable existence for the first five years of their lives, an IQ of more than 80, no history of drug use, and an admitting diagnosis of conduct disorder, as opposed to psychosis.

Of course this does not mean that a child who fails to meet all of these criteria does not stand a chance of success. What it does mean is that even now the potential exists for a more precise diagnostic procedure with the concomitant benefit of being able to earmark certain children for success at the time of admission. Such children at the very outset could be placed on a trajectory that would seek to move them at a predictable pace from one known milestone to another. Aside from the immediate benefit to the child, this would have the larger benefit of creating a demonstrably successful program within the surrounding context of hit-or-miss, trial-and-error, groan-and-give-up.

What about those who are unsuitable candidates for the "success trajectory"? If the system retains its present minimal commitment to real results, there would have to be systematic triage whereby the less promising children receive not our best but our second-best efforts. The term *triage* has unpleasant connotations and goes against the humane principles that have attracted many people to the helping professions. It acquired its present meaning in the French medical corps during World War I when there were not enough doctors and nurses to treat all the wounded at the front. Those with treatable wounds whose lives could be saved were given prompt medical attention, while those with more serious wounds and a questionable prognosis were put aside.

For example, of the males I have worked with who had a history of drug abuse, I have known of only one who was able to kick the habit and move ahead with his life. All the other crack users simply lacked the discipline, self-esteem, hope, and powers of concentration they needed to advance their schooling. As a teacher it pains me to turn my attention away from these students to others with more promise. And if, like a doctor at the front, I were constrained to give such students my second-best efforts, I want the big brass in headquarters to know that an important piece of the job is not getting done and requires a more intensive intervention.

Similarly, the children who have been in foster care since infancy and have traveled from one placement to another generally lack the self-regard and the trust in adults to respond favorably to their schooling. The process of triage would also have to sequester those children with a history of psychosis. They simply are not playing by the same rules as the conduct-disordered, and their response to discipline and B-Mod is unpredictable. Their compliance comes and goes in spurts that follows different patterns from the purely conduct-disordered children. They should be placed in a setting that provides treatment appropriate to their condition— just as a patient with tuberculosis is not thrown together with the candidate for a heart transplant.

At present I have a class of eight conduct-disordered children and one schizophrenic. My psychotic student is on daily medication. Depending on how recently he has eaten, when he receives his medication, and whether he has smoked a joint, his behavior fluctuates between the wildly hyperactive and overpowering somnolence. I prefer the latter as I literally have to stand over him and hold him in his chair when his energy is up. When the need to sleep hits, he will often line up two or three chairs next to each other and recline along them. I am so grateful for this respite that I do nothing to stop him. My conduct-disordered students, however, observe his sleeping preparations with interest and approval. They of course are happy for any chance to take a break from their schooling, and they too start to line up chairs. When this happens my position is not just difficult; it is untenable.

No one is happy with triage, and it is disturbing to watch children who are already in bad shape deteriorate further. My hope is that if the RTCs could predict their successes and turn them out with regularity, funding and resources might then be elevated to a point of parity with the need. Once the folks in the trenches can send a steady stream of healed residents back to headquarters, maybe the brass will send more resources.

If there is a precise method for differential diagnosis, then the term of treatment can be projected accordingly. At present, in the optimal situation—that is, the child had reasonably sound nurture up to the age of five, and did not become seriously oppositional until adolescence—we can hope to do discernible good over a two-year period. We provide a safe environment wherein the child can process the anger that built up immediately prior to placement. We have a school environment that intimates the promise of a better life, and we have staff who are able to help these children overcome their basic distrust and sense of outrage. For such children two years at Leake & Watts is a regenerative experience.

But what about the ones who have been in placement all their lives? What about the ones with psychiatric manifestations? What about the ones who have become drug involved? This comprises fully 80 percent of our present population, and for them two years is utterly inadequate. Given the process that brought them to their present straits, there simply is no two-year fix that is going to put them back on track.

The first question that needs to be asked is whether a child who has been deprived of sufficient nurture from the very beginning can ever be made into an autonomous and competent adult. This is a tough question, and the mental health professionals equivocate. There are hints that, for a person to develop acceptable adult capabilities, there absolutely *must* be stable nurture in the infant years. Whether or not this is true lies beyond the range of my concerns as a teacher. It is a question, however, to which those who create policy for RTCs need a definitive answer. Common sense suggests that if a child whose life has been out of joint for the last couple of years can be put back on track within two years, then the child who has experienced hardship for, say, the past eight years might respond favorably to six or eight years of treatment. There probably is a point of deprivation at which the basic foundation of the personality is so tenuous and undeveloped that the prognosis for real growth becomes exceedingly bleak. For children at this level, the RTC would be forced to create a life-time adult community that could employ the residents to create services or products for the surrounding community. At the turn of the century Leake & Watts ran a farm in upstate New York.

One of the tragedies of the present situation is the way in which the agency terminates the stay of children whose supposed term of treatment has come to an end before they have been able to respond successfully. Last spring, for example, we had a sudden purge of the older students. I recall asking a colleague about one of my students; I was told that he was on a "hit list" of 18-year-olds to be sent away as soon as a new placement could be found. Some of the children on this list had been at the agency for as long as five years. This had been the most regenerative and stabilizing period of their lives, and now the heat was on to send them packing, partially due to their age, but also due to a rising tide of indignation because they had failed to meet their treatment goals.

Had there been a consensus at the time of admission that these children were seriously troubled and would require a six- to eight-year course of treatment, the situation would have been very different. The extended treatment program would have established a succession of realistic short-term goals, some of which would have been met at the end of three or five years. Under such a program the child care staff would not have to struggle with their own sense of failure (which often manifests itself as rancor toward the child) and the child would feel that the time in placement had been productive. What is needed, in short, is a program that is commensurate with the task.

The problem with short-term treatment as presently constituted is that it removes the onus of getting results. If the RTC is viewed as a two-year treatment program wherein structure and B-Mod will straighten out the wayward child, we can take the stand that those who do not make significant improvement over this period are really not suited to our particular program and should be someone else's concern. Implicit in a fixed term of treatment is the realization that there is no fixed goal or mode of treatment. If you want to set a broken leg or cure pneumonia, you allocate as much time as the job requires. Many of these children, having been assigned to an RTC through the courts, perceive their stay as a period of penal servitude, whereas it should be restorative—like going to the hospital.

When a service organization does not track the performance of its former charges, it is due to a general awareness that no news is better than bad news. Anyone who questions the value of systematic follow-up should look at the detailed charts, diagrams, and tables that Healey and Bronner did for delinquent children in Chicago and Boston 70 years ago. They tracked thousands of children and compiled exact figures on recidivism. Some of this information was disquieting and some reassuring, but the researchers knew exactly what they were doing. Our present system is an amorphous machine that ingests a child at one point and then regurgitates him at some later indeterminate point, no questions asked.

Admittedly the work at present is devastating, and I am not sure how I would feel about looking at a bimonthly tally sheet telling me how many of my former students are dead or in jail. In fact, follow-up would be tolerable only in a system in which there was an overt commitment to getting results. When there is an expectation of success one can face failure and reevaluate how the job is being done. If the RTCs had the state's support and a mandate to get the job done, they would want to follow up, as they would start having some good news to report.

This is not to say that there is a swift and easy course of treatment for these children. It is unrealistic to ask for the radical overhaul of social services that would solve all the problems at once; it is not unrealistic, however, especially in small private agencies, to carve out certain areas of endeavor where success and results become predictable certainties rather than random serendipities.

The agency's school is the setting in which I find these children are making the most headway. Prior to working for Leake & Watts I taught in a high school that served a psychiatric hospital for adolescents. The children were not just wild; they were crazy. As a result, the school could be no more than a small appendage on the medical apparatus that was attending to the children. When the work was difficult or impossible the children went off in some schizoid, manic, or depressive realm beyond the pale of rational human discourse. When this happens, a teacher is helpless. There has been a breakdown of the volitional and cognitive faculties upon which learning depends.

At the end of my first year at Leake & Watts I had an experience that caught me entirely by surprise, and the significance of it gradually become more apparent over the next two years. Our valedictorian for the graduation ceremonies was a bright but exceedingly wild and difficult girl. She had engaged the interest and affection of numerous teachers, only to disappoint and frustrate most of them with her impossible behavior. The feeling among most of the staff was that her stay had at best been a mixed experience and she still had a lot to learn about what constitutes adult behavior.

She started off her valedictory address by recounting how much the years at Leake & Watts had meant to her and how much she appreciated the teaching staff and her many friends. Almost at once she started to sob, but she was one of those stalwart beings who was not going to let a few tears stand in the way of saying what was on her mind. She simply pushed ahead, and the more she said the more she wept. As this was going on, an emotional charge began sweeping through the audience. At first a few of her immediate friends started sniffling, and then the contagion took off. By the time she had completed her address, which was no more than three or four minutes, staff, students, and total strangers were weeping out loud, blowing their noses, and wiping away the tears.

For me this was a startling revelation of how powerful the RTC experience can be, even under less-than-ideal conditions. This girl had not responded well to treatment and had eluded and mocked much of the schooling we had tried. Among those shedding tears were teachers who had been saying, only days earlier, "Thank heaven we won't have to struggle with her next year." For all her mischief and opposition, she was able to recognize that her teachers were the ones who had never given up trying to bring out the best in her.

It is in school that the children have the most consistent and satisfying experiences with adults; here is where they are given objectives to achieve. Those who are educators in RTCs must recognize and exploit their therapeutic potential to the fullest. Specifically this means that educators should first and foremost seek to create a powerful and regenerative relationship with their students. It means that they should stress competence first, then remediation. And it means that a major and explicit goal in the curriculum should be to help the students to a positive and viable sense of identity.

The first step toward creating effective bonds with the children is to minimize fragmentation in their lives. Connect them as intensively as possible with the adults in their lives. The school at Leake & Watts equivocates on this. Some classes spend four or five periods with one teacher, while others move about during the day. Of my four years at Leake & Watts I have had a contained class for three years. This means that I am together with the same group for reading the newspaper, making photographs, learning about Martin Luther King, Jr., operating the sewing machine, and watching movies. I feel that this is a reasonably good simulation of life itself. Some of it is disagreeable—spelling tests and reading aloud—while watching movies is restful.

Much of the day we have a VCR in our classroom, and as a group we have watched *Beverly Hills Cop I* and *II* probably half a dozen times. There are many lines that we all know by heart and some of us—myself included—can do a passable imitation of Eddie Murphy's sardonic horse laugh. Another favorite is *Lethal Weapon*, especially the moment when Danny Glover has to subdue his partner, Mel Gibson. As Danny Glover gets up, he shakes off the dust, straightens his coat and tie, and sighs, "Man, I'm too old for this shit." My students shriek with laughter, replay the passage, and exclaim, "Come on, Howe, say it. This is your line." Now whenever I have to forcibly escort one of my students back to his desk, he will say, "Back off, Howe, you're too old for this shit."

It is a real pleasure to spend recreational time with these students. On such occasions I find that I am buying credit that can be applied later on to more routine activities. A couple of years back I had a very enjoyable interlude that extended over a two week period. During the afternoons for the two weeks before Christmas we showed the entire five-part TV serial that was made on the great nineteenth-century tribal chief, Shaka Zulu. I started out with printed handouts about colonial policy, key dates, methods of warfare, and the fate of the Zulu empire, but we ended up just sitting back like a family watching television. Anyone who wanted to make a comment felt free to do so and in fact my students had a lot to say about tribal life, characterization, the landscape, the intransigence of Shaka. At present, activities of this sort tend to occur as interruptions in the academic schedule, sometimes making it difficult to get back to normal. What is needed is more planned and programmatic chunks of recreation whose sole purpose is to put everyone at ease with one another.

Trips and excursions also have a wonderfully cohesive and binding effect. Picnics, cookouts, museum outings, a visit to the local police station—all of these are cozy and amiable experiences. Whenever I take my students on a morning outing—say, to the Natural History Museum—we stop at a public park in Yonkers on the way back for a barbecue. We lay out paper plates, beverages, forks, and condiments and then get food all over our hands and faces. These occasions are also a simulation of family life.

There seldom are problems with the students' behavior on such outings. Occasionally someone will go AWOL if a trip off the grounds goes near familiar haunts. Basically, once the tight constraints of the classroom are lifted, the customary cycle of discipline and non-compliance is suspended.

Once the teacher's therapeutic function is formally recognized, the system should accommodate and support it to the utmost. First, the teachers should receive supervision—not in the sense of administrators peeking through the door to make sure that the class is behaving and busy—but in the sense that therapists have access to other professionals in the field with whom to share their defeats, frustrations, and puzzlements. Once a week a teacher should be able to sit down with a more experienced staff member and simply pour out his concerns. In the volatile environment of the school, I am constantly asking myself, "Did I do the right thing with Alberto?" "Why was Maria so angry with me?" "Did Lenny play me for a fool when I gave him that pass to leave class?" Supervision does not propose to answer such questions; its purpose is to lighten the burden of being vexed by them.

The teachers should receive some training in the clinical and therapeutic dimensions of their work. There should be a much greater appreciation of how profoundly debilitating this work is for a teacher. This was brought home to me with unexpected force a year ago when I took a four-day leave of absence to attend my daughter's wedding in California and Mexico. By making clever use of the weekends and a bootleg day of sick leave I was able to stay away for eight days. I came back tanned, refreshed, and thoroughly rested—I felt like a new person.

My first day back to school it was a bleak Monday morning with a light drizzle. One by one by students trudged into class, dropped their heads on their desks, buried their faces in their overcoats, and went to sleep. I tried to speak with them, but they just grunted and said they wished to be left alone. I passed out trinkets I had bought in Mexico and they dropped them listlessly on the floor beneath their desks. Their depression, incidentally, had nothing to do with my trip. Mondays are frequently awful as those who went home on a weekend pass had a terrible time and those who did not are worried about what they missed. The weight of gloom in the room was absolutely and irresistibly overpowering. By the time it was 9:45 and they left for their third period class, I was depleted beyond words. The cause of my depletion was simply being brought face to face with the depression of my students. Just as their high spirits can be an elixir, their gloom can sink your spirits.

What I had experienced was the fact that the classroom is one of the few places where the children feel at liberty to unload their emotional baggage. In a conventional school a teacher can redirect these concerns to counselors, social workers, and the home. The special ed teacher, however, takes on everything, at least for the duration of the school day. For the students, there is no other person and no other setting to which they can take that particular depression at that particular time. A teacher must find a way to process both his own feelings and those of the students. Lacking a ready and reliable expedient to relieve these feelings, many of us simply shut down. This is not a solution, however, but an outcome. It deprives the students of the attention they require and it leaves the teacher still weighed down by stress and frustration.

I recognize this kind of depletion as an important part of my job, as all I really have to give these children is my concern and energy. But there is no haven or resource in my professional life where I can replace and renew these energies. I see my colleagues, all of whom take the lives of their students seriously, drifting through the school building looking wasted and ravaged. Let the administration of the RTCs take account of this fact and support the teachers in a manner commensurate with the genuinely therapeutic work they are doing.

Beyond the nurturing relationship, the next step is to work at building competence in the children. When I first came to Leake & Watts I was struck by the perversity of taking a group of wild and disruptive kids, placing them in a classroom together, and then telling them to do the very schooling that had been eliciting their worst behavior for the last six to eight years. One succumbs to the prevailing agenda and, as time went by, I put this thought aside. Two years later a new teacher came to the school and started expressing the very same sentiment. I realized that I had not been wrong, but had drifted off into insensibility.

The root of this problem lies in the specific nature of special education. In its classic application the special educator takes a child with an impairment—such as deafness—and finds the means to work through this impairment and convey information. When one is dealing with physiological impairments, this makes sense. The impairment is at the heart of the work and defines the job at hand.

This approach does not translate quite so readily, however, for the conduct-disordered child. Consider the following scenario from a recent summer session. We generally start off the school day by passing out a newspaper to each child. For the past year-and-a-half we had used *The Daily News*, a lurid but readable tabloid. It was decided to switch to *USA Today*, which has a better representation of national and international news. The students had an immediate aversion to it. They could not find what they were looking for, and when they did, they had a hard time understanding it.

A professor of special education, who was also a reading specialist, had been our consultant for the summer. Her advice focused on reading impairment and she proposed that we pass out to each student a mimeographed handout on which to answer questions about what, when, where, and why for each story. If the students were resistant, what they needed was stronger medicine. We had started out with one problem and now we had two: the students were reading a newspaper they did not like supported by a strategy they did not like. An alternative choice would have been to find an easier and more agreeable paper. But to ignore the impairment is to cease to be a special educator whose traditional response is a new remedial trick. With students whose cognitive difficulties are due to an oppositional attitude and low self-esteem, however, you simply switch back to *The Daily News*, which is what we finally did.

Although we cannot afford to overlook the weaknesses of these children in math and language skills, we must take care not to let remediation degenerate into a blunt instrument with which to obtain submission. The students are often made to feel that our only thought is, "if you can't learn to convert fractions, you will never get a job and make a living." There is a very fine line that needs to be drawn and redrawn all the time between the work they need but loathe and the more agreeable work that may not address their limitations. It would require a delicate procedure that would be fine-tuned individually for each student. The first step would be to assess each student's strengths and then engage those strengths as fully as possible. If this first step brings the savor of success and achievement, then on the backswing one can take on the remediation of traditional academic skills.

Clearly, vocational training would be a strong component in such a program. In New York City over 25,000 jobs open up every year that do not require a high school diploma. These are not just the menial tasks of houseworkers and janitors, but skilled jobs such as machine-tool operators, stone cutters, cosmetologists, file clerks, and photo lab technicians, all of which pay above the minimum wage and have opportunities for advancement. An RTC school needs to provide its students with hands-on professional training that will nourish their self-respect. Then one can get on with the business of remediation without making the students feel they are being babied. With tasks such as setting up portrait lighting, taking pictures, doing darkroom work or soldering electric circuits the students take obvious pleasure in learning age-appropriate skills.

A further step toward fostering competence would be to identify the more capable students and provide them with high-level individual instruction. Traditionally, American education has favored the impaired student and has assumed that the brighter ones will do just fine. This has been recognized as lopsided, and the result has been the many programs for the gifted. Special educators need to think less about impairment and more about ability. A student whose reason for being in special education is opposition and bad behavior may yet have superior intellectual abilities.

At present we are happy to provide a one-on-one reading tutorial for those students of high school age who are reading on a second- or third-grade level. I have occasionally suggested that we should try Shakespeare one-on-one with students who are reading at a post high school level. Unfortunately, most professionals in special education cannot envision the implementation of such a tutorial. They cannot get beyond the paradox of special education for the gifted. It is essential, however, that, along with all the remedial travail, there be evidence of high-level work being done by those who have the ability. Most students feel disgraced and degraded by their placement in an RTC and in special education. Their language arts books have pictures of little children playing catch, and their math work books are page after page of the same addition, subtraction, multiplication, and division problems they have been doing for the last six years.

The third major component in the educational program would be a forceful and systematic emphasis on self-regard and identity. The education of these children is gravely impeded by their fragmentary perception of a plausible adult identity. An essential step to their emergence from adolescence is to form an appropriate career goal. When I ask my students what they would like to do in life, they will generally have a ready-made answer about the military or the post office. These are simply stock answers that are proffered in response to a stock question. Hopeful and realistic answers to these questions, however, arise in a sound and nurturing home. These students are aware of this lack in their lives, and beneath their automatic responses about the armed services or the police force there lies a ravenous avidity for an adult identity.

I had an interesting experience last year with a student who was desperately grasping toward an adult identity. As we came into the spring quarter last year, it became clear, to everyone's surprise, that one of my students—an 18-year-old with an awful mouth and an ill-governed temper—was going to graduate. He had entertained a variety of grandiose plans for college and the military, but they were precluded by his sixth-grade reading level. His senior social worker arranged for me to take him to a vocational school that is run by the Bulova Watch Company. Here he could learn watch repair, jewelry making, computer repair, or small electronic repair. We were given a tour of the place where he saw people very much like himself—rough and street smart—working with soldering irons, oscilloscopes, and voltage meters; he was transfixed. It simply had never occurred to him in a concrete way that there was real work waiting to be done by his likes.

On the way back to Leake & Watts he began thinking out loud about what subjects he would take, where he would live, how he would save money, what he would do when his schooling was complete. For the first time ever he was looking at a plausible trajectory into adult life. The moment he got back to the agency he started telling his friends and within three days several of them approached the same social worker about getting an appointment to visit the Bulova School.

But this is not the end of the story. My student had decided that he wanted to enter the training program at Bulova for computer repairs. When he went back for testing, however, he did not qualify, but he did qualify for small electronics. Far from being disappointed, he was delighted. Having spent all of two weeks in my class doing occasional light soldering, he felt that he was already something of an expert. His brief and superficial experience had been sufficiently engaging to leave him with a sense of competence. Imagine if we had taken this boy aside two years earlier when he was admitted and told him what his parents had never told him: "We've got career plans for you and we are going to start making an expert out of you right now." His work in soldering would not have been just another desultory experience. It would have been a solid pre-vocational experience that would have given a focus and purpose to his remaining schooling.

There is a tendency to tell these children that until they can write a complete sentence or reduce a fraction, there is no need to clutter up their lives with a lot of useless baggage about careers. A career then becomes something remote and inaccessible that can be attained only by traversing long and odious tracts of decimals and fifth-grade readers. The prospect of this journey only reinforces the student's worst fear—that a career is not for him.

Another obstacle for these students in the path to a positive self-image is the lack of powerful and persuasive images of black identity in the world around them. With children who already have a problem of low or undeveloped self-esteem, it would be a worthy goal to help them see their color as an asset rather than a liability.

They are able to feel genuine admiration for Martin Luther King, Jr., and Harriet Tubman. Beyond the handful of biographies of distinguished blacks, there needs to be a forceful and credible curriculum on all aspects of black culture. I have made sporadic attempts to teach about Hannibal, the Harlem Renaissance, Malcolm X, Islam, and the great empires of Africa. Basically it has been too fragmentary and too extraneous. There has been nothing in their previous schooling to prepare them to receive and process a body of information about black culture. This is a deficiency that reaches down to the roots of educating black Americans, and it will require intensive and thoughtful labor to correct it.

Recently I was both amused and touched by what must be a common experience in the lives of my students. We were watching a movie in which Chuck Norris was single-handedly winning the war we had lost in Vietnam. One of my students turned to me and remarked, "I am sick of seeing skinny white boys kicking ass all over the world." I was reminded how different the experience of watching Shaka Zulu had been. The bulk of the film is about tribal life—warfare, rivalries, marriage, bonds of kinship—and they found the entire ten hours thoroughly absorbing and rewarding. This was a chance to see black people going about their lives with dignity and self-determination. Interestingly, there were loud hoots and groans at the moment when Shaka signed over to the British the land that was to become Natal. These children had never had a lesson on colonial history, but they knew very well what was happening.

The changes I envisage under the rubric of education are attainable under present conditions. To implement them would require a broader therapeutic commitment on the part of special ed schools than is now the case. Since, however, the rank-and-file teachers are already deeply involved with the well-being of their students, the therapeutic inclination is already present. If the RTCs and the schools within them were to guarantee certain predictable results, the nature of the task would change both for staff and residents. It would not be unrealistic, for example, to earmark certain students for graduation the day they arrive—even though it might be as few as 20 percent. Some students could be assigned to a fixed career trajectory at the age of fifteen. This could be anything from carpentry to computer repairs. There would then be the appropriate three- or four-year apprenticeship to ensure this outcome.

At present all of us who work with these children are staggering under the weight of lowered expectations and compromised standards. There is little likelihood that this chain of defeat will snap at the top where policy is made, far from the arena of struggle and engagement. There is, however, the possibility at some point much further down the chain, where individual staff are dealing with individual children, that the agenda, the expectations, and the results could be radically reevaluated. Any agency or school that could turn out a steady trickle of promising young adults on a regular and predictable basis would immediately establish a benchmark for the system as a whole.

9

What Keeps Me Going

I have now been teaching the children at Leake & Watts for almost four years, and the experience has filled me with conflicting feelings. The children have voracious needs and they have forceful and abrupt ways of making them known. I am often exhausted, angry, or depressed, but I am never bored. If I am to continue in this work, I need to be convinced at some level that it is worth all the strain. At present my professional life stands under the shadow of unresolved stress and growing areas of stultification, both of which are offset by the deep sense of engagement I feel with the problems, the pain, and the unflagging impudence of the children.

One of the things I have not relished is getting used to my life as a school teacher. Much that is wrong with our educational system as a whole derives from the low esteem, failed expectations, and extreme stress of being a teacher. This is as true for the mainstream classroom as it is for the special education classroom. There can be little doubt that the stress of being a solitary teacher standing up before a class of 30 adolescents in a public high school is comparable to my hardship in a class of eight conduct-disordered students with a teaching aide at my side. For both, not only is the classroom a place of stress and frustration; once you leave the classroom you are constantly reminded of the low professional station of the school teacher. This is not so much a matter of pay which, if prorated over the relative brevity of the school day and the school year, works out to a decent middle class wage. But in matters of teaching style and content, accountability, and professional autonomy, the school teacher is a menial.

A school teacher stands in marked contrast to the professor, who is generally perceived as a high-level professional. The professor's work takes place in the realm of intellect, which, in American universities, is exempt from outside interference. The actual number of teaching hours is scandalous by the standards of the work world: as little as six hours a week in a prestige university, while nine to twelve hours a week is the norm. Moreover, society is prepared to acknowledge the professor's expertise and highly trained skills. In the case of the school teacher, the opposite is true in all areas. The school teacher is a low-level professional; the training is of a dull and pedestrian nature and is viewed with suspicion by all but professional educators; the teacher is subject to constant interference, observation, clock-punching, and generally inimical attention.

Now in my fifth year as a school teacher, I still do not know how I am able to be in class with students for seven periods a day. Ours is a typical school schedule: an eight-period day with one free prep period for each teacher. When you see a teacher supine on the couch in the teachers' lounge or drooping like a zombie over a cup of coffee, you can assume it is prep time. One is simply too wiped out to use the time to update the grade book or produce new lesson materials for the classroom.

Going to the bathroom is an event that must be planned well in advance and such work-a-day liberties as calling the gas company to check about the bill, or making a dental appointment, require significant preparation. As in the business world, your time is accounted for every minute of the day. The difference is the unremitting attention that is required. There is absolutely nothing like being thrown into a classroom with a group of children for whom one possesses absolute accountability for the time they are with you. When you close the door behind you and the last student enters your class, there is an intensity of expectation from which there is no deliverance until the class is over and the door opens again. The ensuing 40-minute performance in which you convey material, create an atmosphere of expectation, and struggle for the attention of the students is incomparable. This of course is one of the givens of being a teacher, and those who do not get some kind of kick out of this particular experience, grueling as it is, are in the wrong profession.

Unfortunately it is axiomatic in human services that the professionalism is most compromised at the point where the services are actually delivered. When you get to the point where staff meets child, whether it is a teacher with students or a case worker with a case load, the rules of the game are often in a state of intolerable flux. For the teacher who has been assigned a class of unmanageable children with cognitive skills spanning a range of six or eight grades, professional aims and skills are meaningless and one must temporize, fudge, and fly by the seat of the pants. The same is true for a social worker who is assigned an impossible case load.

The higher up the ladder you are, the greater your right to find job satisfaction. Thus in an RTC the psychology PhDs possess high-level skills which they are at liberty to deploy in a productive and intelligent manner: they assess cognitive functioning and personality deficits. The consummation of their labors will be a single-spaced three page document to guide social workers, cottage staff, and teachers in assigning tasks and gauging results. If the tasks come to naught and the results are negligible, the performance of the psychologist is in no way compromised. They are functional professionals who are doing what they were trained to do. The same is true for the administrators. Their job is to obtain compliance and performance from middle-class professionals who subscribe to the middle-class ethic of trying to please the boss.

It pains me to see the menial status of teachers in terms of petty accountability. The teachers I now know, both colleagues at Leake & Watts and friends who work in the New York City public schools, constantly come under the heavy hand of management. They must present a weekly lesson plan in which they inform the administration exactly what they intend to do for every period of the day, every day of the week. Although I am exempt from having to punch a clock, this is common practice in many schools. And one is subject to constant censure for small matters of technique and style. The response of the administration may be that with the calibre of people now in teaching, they must be watched every step of the way. If this is really so, then in the interest of the teachers,

the students, and the profession as a whole, the quality and education of teachers must be upgraded to the point where they no
longer need to be badgered and harassed by their superiors.

The majority of school teachers do not last long—I was recently at a seminar sponsored by the New York Board of Education
where it was announced that the average term of service is now
four years. And yet despite the many affronts to one's self-regard
and the frantic quality of the time spent in the classroom, a surprising number of teachers are able to look beyond all these hard-
ships and recognize their task as a vocation taken up on behalf of
their students. These are the ones gifted with the ability to keep
alive their hope and patience. Year after year they remain open to
the needs of their students, they continue to view teaching as a
privileged calling, and they give more than they get back in return.
I sense three such anointed teachers in our school at present: Miss
K., the math teacher across the hall from me; Miss C., the eighth-
grade teacher in the room next to mine; and Miss S., our reading
specialist. All three are old-timers in the field—five years quali-
fies—and yet they continue to be affectionate, hopeful, and concerned.

The youngest, Miss K., a woman still in her twenties, has
found in math a subject that is concrete and specific. It is the
subject to which our students are least resistant, as it is devoid of
emotional content. When they refuse all other academic work,
they will often find solace and peace in solving problems. Miss K.
is able to engage the children with sympathy and patience, behind
which her intention to teach math is always visible. She is one of
those cited by our returning alumni for sticking to the subject and
trying to teach.

The eighth-grade teacher, Miss C., has been in special education for 20 years. She has made both an art and a science of
creating a classroom atmosphere that is at once controlled and
supportive. With unflagging patience she reiterates her expectations, and over a period of time—it can take as much as five
months—her students come to accept these expectations and temper their behavior. Her room then becomes something of a sanc-
tuary in which her students are able to put aside their habitual need
to misbehave.

The reading teacher, Miss S., has been in special education
for over 10 years. She goes about her work with fine precision. She
is able to assess exactly what a student's weaknesses in reading are,

and then she will embark on a course of remediation addressed specifically to these weaknesses. The pleasure she takes in her student's progress sustains both her and them.

Within the chaos and frustration of working with such students, these three teachers have been able to identify objectives that are commensurate with their students' needs and their own abilities. Above all, however, they have been able to maintain an even-minded patience and singularity of purpose. For all of this to work out requires a degree of patience, self-knowledge, and natural kindness that one does not often encounter.

I admire this attainment as one that still stands beyond my reach. In this regard the career of a teacher can be seen as a lifelong apprenticeship in hope and patience. Since the teaching profession would be impoverished without these inspired achievers, I would hope that the teachers' colleges would do more to awaken a sense of vocation, while the schools themselves would endeavor to nurture and sustain it.

The spectre of burnout awaits those whose sense of calling falters and who are unable to assign their energies within realistic limits. It occurs when a job exerts pressure to lower one's hopes and expectations. For example, a teacher finds herself spending more and more time on behavior problems and less and less on instruction. The children are not responding to attempts at discipline and they are refusing to make use of what little they have learned. All the while the administration is expressing its disapproval of the teacher's style of classroom management.

One of two things can then happen. One leaves in dismay, saying, "My principles and ideals will not allow me to stay on and do the work in a compromised manner." Or, having readjusted one's hopes and expectations, one stays on the job while putting forth guarded or minimal exertion. In the latter case there has been some internal breakdown and one lacks the commitment and energy that were there at the beginning. For those who readjust and stay put, burnout, far from being a terminal condition, can be the first step toward professional advancement. The teacher who had once been filled with enthusiasm to give her students a love for lyric poetry may discover a new enthusiasm to become an assistant principal. In the process, however, something important has been lost. The newly appointed assistant principal is not just a resourceful survivor; she is also someone who has been able to relinquish or compromise her ideals.

This instance represents a process that is constantly at work in the human-service fields. The administrative echelon will consist to a great extent of former enthusiasts who were able to accommodate the disappointments of the system. If the lower echelon consists of crumbling idealists while the seasoned pros who have survived the demise of their ideals are calling the shots, this will influence the way in which things are done. This may be a desirable situation in fields such as real-estate development or bond sales, where raw idealism can lead to unwise risks and financial mismanagement. In the human services, however, where ideals support a personal investment and high expectations, the work becomes cynical and depersonalized under the leadership of a cadre of "realists." In an RTC this can mean that there is a basic disinclination coming down from above when it comes to personalizing the work or entertaining high expectations.

Last year I had a typical incident of the kind that can separate the survivors from the struggling novices. One of my students was scheduled to take the New York State competency test in mathematics and was terrified. His proficiency was absolutely marginal and failure would mean no high school diploma. When the time came to go to the room where the test was being offered, he refused to leave my classroom. I started pleading with him, first in my classroom and then out in the hall, as he had decided to return to his cottage. He kept trying to walk off and I kept trying to propel him in the direction of the test. This turned into something of a commotion that was noted by one of the assistant principals and one of the teachers. They looked on for a while with weary amusement and then both said approximately the same thing. "Forget it, Howe. If he doesn't want to take the test that's his business."

I did not pay much attention to this advice and after much back and forth and dramatic pleading, my student went off to the designated room, took the test, and passed by one point. The assistant principal who had spoken to me earlier drew me aside and said, "You can't go on like that. You'll burn yourself out. And he probably would have taken the test anyway." I suspect that she was right about his taking the test anyway, and yet I would hold out for a system that allows and even encourages some degree of emotional profligacy. These children have been so starved for any degree of emotional investment in their lives: a humane system could take some steps to make good this deficiency.

There is one aspect of burnout from which I do not believe

anyone is fully exempt: disaffection toward the client. This can be episodic or it can become a permanent condition. Year after year a teacher struggles with reluctant students; a drug counselor treats addicts who will not kick their habit; a therapist takes on clients who cling to their maladaptive ways. I am now in my fourth year of having students shout every possible obscenity into my face and hurl carefully thought-out assignments on the floor, exclaiming, "Get this shit off my desk."

The professional response is for me to recognize these outbursts as displaced anger for which I am just a surrogate target. The reality is that my students bring real anger to these exchanges and I invest real feelings in their education. Many of us in the helping professions like to imagine that we have an inexhaustible store of good will and patience. In my life as a teacher, however, I am not engaged in mock battles that take place in an emotional vacuum. My feelings are battered and at times I feel my anger rising to meet that of my students.

It is disquieting to witness the erosion of one's own charitable resources, and I find myself trying to deny or reinterpret my feelings toward the children. I see the resentment of my colleagues erupting in oblique and unexpected directions. I often hear staff say, "It's not the kids that bother me. It's the administration." This is an evasion, the real meaning of which is clear. Recently a teacher who has struggled to maintain a patient and generous relationship with his students got into a fist fight with another staff member over a meaningless trifle.

After four years I am still willing to have a student with me in my classroom during my lunch break or during my prep period, but that willingness is not what it used to be. Both for my own sake and for the sake of my students, I wish that agencies such as Leake & Watts could provide the staff support that would help me to acknowledge and mitigate these inevitable developments.

A principal advantage in the battle of burnout is age. When a 25-year-old undertakes this kind of work, the expectations are apt to be sky-high, while the ability to absorb defeat and frustration will take another 20 years to develop. A significant number of my colleagues have started this work as a second career and, although they still bear the full stress and depletion the work brings, they have the ability to distinguish between the possible and the impossible. They have come to terms with their own abilities and achievements. They know who they are and they know why they allow themselves to be abused by the children. They recognize the inevitability of sparse and hard-won results, and they have the self-awareness to experience failure without feeling that their own person has been diminished in the process.

Under present conditions the course of advancement in this work is one that tends to take a person out of the trenches and back behind the lines to the command post. This means that the teacher who is trying to maintain her personal involvement and high expectations is constantly subject to the siren call of administrative work. In the helping professions the only trench soldier I know of who enjoys prestige and a decent paycheck is the psychiatrist working in a mental hospital. Otherwise the steps to advancement are marked by increasingly remote and diluted involvement with the children. Two job changes at our school over the past year neatly illustrate this progression. Our senior teacher in the high school was promoted from her classroom to an office where she does educational assessment and curriculum development. Prior to this she had been in charge of the computer room which already represents a somewhat mediated contact with the children. The slot that she vacated in the computer room has now been taken over by our second senior teacher.

Beyond this, the actual physical structure of the school building declares that advancement moves away from the students to safer and more fortified positions. Thus, the teachers are assigned to a classroom with open doors through which students pass at will. The low-level administrators have offices with locked doors through which a student passes only at the pleasure of the occupant. And then our principal is separated from the students by two doors and a secretary. Finally, at the summit of the educational edifice, is our director of education who is in an entirely different building, also separated from the outside world by a secretary and two doors.

What we do for our administration is of course no different from what the Bank of America and General Motors do for theirs. There is nothing intrinsically wrong with this. Obviously a high-level administrator cannot have rowdy students passing in and out of his office. What is unfortunate, however, is the inescapable impression that proximity to the students signifies low status. Would it not be more fitting if the senior teachers were given an office with such high-level amenities as a desk, a telephone, and book shelves? And while these senior teachers are in their studies reading, thinking, and counseling individual students, the principal might be in a classroom offering a course for one period a day.

One is especially conscious of the separation between the troops and the brass when called to an administrative office to help put together data on a student. I will enter a room in which psychologists, administrators, and educational evaluators are sitting around a table strewn with bagels, coffee cups, and papers. They are enjoying a break between finishing up one student and starting on the one assigned to my class.

What I would wish for teachers is a course of advancement that acknowledges them as high-level professionals. This tendency is underway in some school districts where "master teachers" exist and the top of the pay scale is creeping over the $50,000-a-year mark. Meanwhile, everybody loses—teachers, taxpayers, parents, and students—if so many low and mid-level teachers are looking for an escape hatch to a more prestigious and less frantic environment.

Twice over my four years I have seen teacher burnout take the form of collapse of the will. There are those teachers who always will enjoy children, who like being in the classroom, do not want to leave the field, but no longer have the strength to impose their will on the students. The two teachers in whom I saw this happen had been in the field for many years and enjoyed their work. They simply did not have the stomach to direct or discipline the students any longer, and at the end of the school year they both left for other jobs.

Ultimately this experience was detrimental for the students. First, students who have passed through an entire year without any significant demands being made will not adjust well to another teacher with more forceful expectations. Second and more important, these students will view the absence of volitional confrontation as a lack of concern. To the extent that these children have experienced direction in their lives, it has generally been gruff and forceful. If a person cannot take the trouble to get tough with them, they will reason that the person probably does not really care for them. And in fact the staff for whom they have the highest regard are the ones who are unflinchingly forceful and loving at the same time.

A couple of years ago I experienced a similar failure of the will. I was having an extremely difficult time with a matter outside the school and it finally depleted me of the energy to oppose my students. I started showing movies in the afternoons and allowed the students to move ahead with their work at whatever pace suited them. They did not exactly know how to say, "Why aren't you on our backs," but they did sense that an element of concern and commitment was missing. They clearly did not like it and such control as I had possessed earlier began to slip away. After a couple of weeks and a Christmas vacation I regained the drive to move ahead with business as usual, but it took another month after that to re-engage the students and convince them that I had the will to fight them on behalf of their education.

One of the most insidious aspects of doing impossible work is the growing stultification that erodes the acuity of one's judgment and perceptions. Stultification is an adaptive response that happens to everyone in this kind of work whereby they become "stupid" in their evaluation of what is really happening. When stultification becomes pervasive and habitual, the result is that large areas of endeavor are either ignored or are erroneously perceived. This is done as a means of preserving a sense of one's own competence. There are ways in which I find that my grasp of reality has shifted ground, and I sense that I am not as smart about things as I used to be.

Last spring I was at a treatment conference for a student from my core group. These meetings are attended by social workers, clinicians, residential staff, and teaching staff. We are all asked to report on how the child is doing and the social worker tries to form a clear composite picture. I started describing the difficulty the child was having in performing at her potential. Since she was an exceptionally bright girl, the clinician sensed that something might be amiss. She started asking about the composition of the class and the abilities of the other students. I reported that the age range was from 14 to 18, that the reading level ran from second grade to post high school, that the IQ range was from 57 to 106, and that there was one girl—the child in question—to seven boys. With a theatrical gesture, the clinician exclaimed, "Good Lord, Howe, that's absurd. How do you expect to do any teaching in a class like that?" She had recognized that with the range of ages, cognitive ability, and reading skills along with the lopsided gender ratio, I was presiding over a room where I simply was not going to accomplish anything.

I gazed at her blankly and came back with some snappy rejoinder such as, "Gee, I never thought of that." This is stultification: the mind is overwhelmed by the many absurdities and compromises it must process. I had so much vexation simply being in the classroom and trying to manage at least a simulation of teaching that I lacked the strength and inclination to analyze my situation. As a step toward maintaining at least a modicum of stability, the mind simply retreats and screens out some of the more disorderly parts of the picture.

In order to approach a problem in an intelligent and resourceful way, one needs to have a mind that is open to possibilities. In work that is as frustrating and difficult as this, the available supply of possibilities often seems to be shrinking. And as a consequence the mind will range in smaller and smaller circles.

This process is pervasive and it hits all of us. One of the destructive results is that a typical response to any new intervention, remedy, or theory is going to be, "Yes, but . . ." When I first started at Leake & Watts, like any new employee, I made a great nuisance of myself by running around to various clinicians, social workers, and administrators announcing, "I've got a good idea." The scenario was always the same. They would hear me out indulgently and then say, "Yes, but . . ."

In one instance, I was struck by the accuracy of our testing of the cognitive and academic abilities of the children. Essentially as a project to amuse and inform myself I ran the IQ scores, grade level, WRAT scores, age, and standardized reading scores through a computer. I found some interesting correlations and it struck me that we could get a fuller prognosis of how these children would perform than was currently available. I demonstrated the program to a couple of administrative colleagues suggesting how we might use it. They all responded with, "Yes, but . . ." "Yes, but the test scores are unreliable, as they are so influenced by how the children feel on the day they are taking the test." "Yes, but the behavior problems are so pervasive that we have no sound basis for prognosis." "Yes, but in a school as small as ours differential treatment is at best a limited option."

All of these are half-truths, but not one of them is a full truth. After an extended period of defeat and frustration, the ability to process new ideas atrophies. This, incidentally, is a vital fact for anyone to keep in mind who intends to reform a system where there is a high level of frustration and failure. The forces of change must be brought to bear from without, as those who are actually doing the work have narrowed their view to the few small areas where they are experiencing success.

This tendency to shut out failure leads to another kind of stultification whereby one simply refuses to contemplate the areas that are not succeeding. This is a perfectly normal and healthy strategy for survival. A competent person with reasonable self-regard is going to be rendered ineffectual if all he does is stare failure in the face. As a consequence, workers will become exceedingly generous in how they assess the outcome of their exertions, and they will overlook their failed efforts or interpret them out of existence.

My own lapse into this defense was brought home at a recent treatment conference. We were talking about a 16-year-old girl who had elevated her reading level from fifth grade to sixth grade, who was attending classes regularly, who was making her bed in the morning and doing her cottage chores. We were all taking turns complimenting one another on a job well done when our revery was interrupted by a new social-work supervisor who exclaimed, "I don't believe what I am hearing. We're talking about a kid who will never graduate from high school, who has no career plans, who has no skills for making a living, and who clings to the staff around here as though she were six years old. And you're talking about what a great job you've done!" I see this social worker regularly at treatment conferences and admire her undaunted will not to lose sight of reality. I have to ask myself, however, how long she can hold on like this.

When you work in a field that is plagued by failure and frustration, even a small dose of self-irony can do you in. I very much admired but could never emulate one of the professors of psychiatry at my previous job. He was a brilliant and learned man for whom everything took an ironic twist. I once remarked to one of the younger residents how fortunate he was to receive instruction from this man. He agreed, but with some hesitation, averring that the man's self-irony was an almost fatal flaw. A typical case presentation would proceed as follows.

> When I was treating patient Jane Doe, it turned out that we had the wrong diagnosis. We decided on a course of treatment that was ill-suited both to the initial erroneous diagnosis and the later correct one. She was totally unresponsive to treatment and after three years we discharged her as incurable. The

last I heard she was fully recovered and living with her mother
in Toledo. Are there any questions?

This is slicing through stultification with a vengeance, but the
blade will inevitably slice the wielder. In my years at Leake &
Watts I have lost much of the reckless assurance that enables
self-disparagement. I fancy that I am not yet fully enveloped by
stultification, but I can feel its inexorable advance.

Another form of professional demise that is less pernicious
than burnout is cognitive dissonance. This is a term employed by
motivational psychologists to describe the discomfort one feels
when knowledge is out of step with reality. There will, for example, be cognitive dissonance for a psychiatrist who believes that
therapy is the only hope for psychotic patients, but finds himself
working for a hospital that does nothing but lobotomies. When a
Marxist discovers that his girlfriend has become an investment
banker, he will experience cognitive dissonance. Where there is
dissonance one seeks to reduce it and achieve consonance. The
psychiatrist will try to convince his medical director to introduce
therapy as an alternative treatment. The Marxist will tell his girlfriend she should be working with the homeless. At the same time
one seeks to avoid situations that aggravate dissonance. The psychiatrist goes to work for a hospital that relies exclusively on therapy and the Marxist finds a new girlfriend at a protest in front of
the Exxon building.

Cognitive dissonance can be a powerful force for career
change, resignation, and acute discomfort while still on the job. In
my own case my knowledge tells me that the work must be intensively personal and of long duration. The reality of the system,
however, dictates that the work be depersonalized and segmented.
When faced with this kind of cognitive dissonance, I have a variety of options. I can try to find opportunities to make the work
more personal and less episodic. I can ask the school to give me a
contained class rather than a sequence of different students coming
to me. Beyond this I can try to isolate myself from information and
experience that may be disquieting. And finally, should the dissonance become too intense, I can seek employment in a setting
where the procedures are more in accord with my views.

This is much less destructive than burnout, as personal commitment and high expectations can survive the pressure of cognitive dissonance. The worker leaves, his hopes and ideals still intact.

Then, unlike the burnt-out teacher, who stays put with lowered hopes and expectations, he can go on trying to do the work as he thinks it should be done.

This year I had the kind of experience that can deliver a terminal blow to one's willingness to go on working in this field. I was assigned a class whose opposition and anger simply outweighed my ability to impose order and direction. Total loss of control can happen a day at a time to anyone; this is when you go home with a crashing headache and go to sleep at four in the afternoon. If, however, this goes on for weeks on end, one experiences an internal breakdown. Since I have been at Leake & Watts I have seen four teachers end up in the hospital after their health collapsed in the face of rising chaos.

Day after day I was unable to bring my class under control. At the worst of times, half of my students would be out in the hall attracting the unfavorable attention of the administration, while the other half was racing around the room refusing all instruction. At the best of times, half the class would be busy, but there would still be four or five students cursing, threatening to fight, and shouting down my attempts to teach. Once this goes on for a couple of weeks the students recognize that they have gained the upper hand, and then instruction takes place only at their pleasure.

I started having insomnia and minor flus in October and November. Then my teaching aide went on maternity leave and I was on my own for an entire month. I have never experienced anything like the sinking feeling of collapse, impotence, and stress that went on for the next couple of months. I would awaken at three in the morning with clenched teeth and dreading the dawn. I mentioned this in passing to a colleague, who said that the teacher who had this group last year had the same experience. When Christmas vacation came, I was sick with a cold which quickly became laryngitis and bronchitis. Never having taken a sick day in my entire four years at Leake & Watts, I started missing days in January.

At the end of January the tide finally turned for me. I was given a replacement teaching aide, and two of my most difficult students left to be replaced by more docile ones. I must ask myself, however, whether any job is worth this kind of assault on one's well-being.

What is it that brings people back year after year for more of the same grueling punishment? For me and many of the staff there is an almost addictive fascination with the children. Their energy level, their reckless sense of play, the pathos of their lives, and their flagrant disregard for all manners and conventions can be a tremendous stimulant. These are the children who have said everything one ever wanted to say.

In my previous school there was an extremely rowdy girl who would go off into fits of intemperate abuse. Once, she was having such a fit in the hall when the principal was passing through. The principal drew herself up to her full height and exclaimed, "I am the principal of this school. I will not tolerate this kind of language in my building. Stop at once."

The student fell to her knees and, like a pagan bowing before an idol, she rocked back and forth with outstretched arms and intoned, "O Great One, I have offended you. Please grant your forgiveness." The principal was struck dumb and looked around for a couple of teachers to extricate her. There was no one there, however, as we had all retreated to our classrooms where we were exploding with laughter.

In my present school the children are tougher and more aggressive. Every year during Black History Month we have a formal lunch for the entire agency, children and staff, with traditional southern cooking. We gathered in the agency dining room and sat family style, eight to a table. The kitchen staff served up a tasty meal of ham hocks and collard greens. Between the main course and the dessert one of the senior administrators tapped his glass for our attention and then offered an eloquent tribute to the chef. He turned to the chef to come forward to acknowledge our thanks and in the two seconds it took the chef to get from the side of the room to the center, a wiry 11-year-old from Brooklyn with fast fists and a firecracker mouth blurted out, "Man, that shit was nasty." The solemnity of the moment was destroyed and smiles swept across the room.

Many of the staff who choose to work with these children find something appealing in their reckless will to rebel. For all of us who have a lingering indignation over the many rules and authority figures we have had to endure, these children speak the unspeakable and quicken the spirit.

Beyond the high jinks and the abusive language there is a gripping intensity to this work. The children are subject to mood swings, depressions, and fits of anger that command one's full attention. The experience of soothing a child who is having a temper tantrum, or comforting a child who is overwhelmed by depression, is unique. There is no certainty that one will succeed, and one's efforts are generally resisted. And yet, when you step into the maelstrom of these children's emotions, there can be no question of what you are doing and why you are doing it. It is obviously true that many people go into this work out of a desire to be needed, and there is nothing contemptible in this. The children embody an unremitting need for human attention, and for those of us who worry about the insubstantiality of most of the world's work, here is an answer.

I count the days until the school vacations, and then find myself back on the grounds before school reopens. I recall last year when we had our February break, I went back on the school grounds within two days, ostensibly to pick up something from my classroom. Everywhere I was met by throngs of rowdy children who told me that the hall monitor had already been on the grounds two hours earlier.

Beyond the emotional rush that comes from being with these children, the life of a teacher is an extraordinary apprenticeship toward the cultivation of certain primal human qualities. For Teilhard de Chardin, teaching is profoundly religious, for it advances the fallen and defective world toward its inevitable perfection. For Plato, teaching is the ultimate act of love, for it is the means by which we propagate the existence of our highest values. And, while that is happening, I am convinced that the teacher is undergoing a greater transformation than the student.

Index